Pictorial History Of The

John and Alice Durant

Pictorial History Of The

AMERICAN CIRCUS

John and Alice Durant

Published by

A. S. BARNES AND COMPANY • New York

BOUND IN HANDCRAFTED MISSION LEATHER BY

BROWN AND BIGELOW, Saint Paul, Minnesota

Contents

Acknowledgments

The authors are deeply indebted to Mrs. Vivienne Mars and Mrs. Goldie Steel of the Harry Hertzberg Circus Collection in the San Antonio Public Library for their guidance, encouragement and invaluable assistance from their historical records in the preparation of this book. We also wish to express particular gratitude to Tom Parkinson of the *Billboard* for his contributions and willingness to help; to Carl H. (Pop) Haussman for the many photographs he prepared for our use; to Ken Mayo of Ringling Brothers Press Department and to the Cristiani family for their cheerful cooperation.

In addition to those mentioned above we are greatly indebted to the following individuals for their help in supplying pictures and information:

Edward August, United Press Photos

George Brinton Beal

Bill Ballantine

Clarence S. Brigham, American Antiquarian Society

Arthur Carleson, New York Historical Society

Alexander P. Clark and Mrs. Herbert McAneny, Princeton University Library

Ernest S. Dodge, Peabody Museum of Salem

Bob Dover, Ringling Brothers

Barbara Fairchild, Cristiani Brothers Circus

Freddie Freeman, Ringling Brothers

Ford Green, San Antonio

J. Y. (Doc) Henderson, Ringling Brothers

Alex Hoag, San Antonio

Dr. Chester Hoyt, Circus Hall of Fame

Lawrence R. Jake, Sarasota

Louis C. Jones, New York State Historical Association

Milton Kaplan and Carl E. Stange, Library of Congress

Peter B. Marien, Brown & Bigelow

Ralph Miller and May Seymour, Museum of the City of New York

Earl Moore, Sarasota

William Mortenson and Saro J. Riccardi, New York Public Library

Marian Murray, John and Mable Ringling Museum of Art

Henry Ringling North

Mary J. Reardon, Harvard College Library

Homer Register, Paul Anderson Co., San Antonio

The *Sabrejets* (Dick Anderson, Juan Rodriguez and Billy Ward)

Joseph Janney Steinmetz, Sarasota

James G. Strobridge, Strobridge Lithographing Co., New York

The Wallendas, Sarasota

Stan Windhorn, *Sarasota Herald Tribune*

Introduction

Since the first wagon show trundled out of nowhere to parade down the street, townsfolk have been intrigued by circuses, not only for the performances but also for the romance and mystery that surround the traveling aggregations. Who knows where circuses go, or how many there are, or who owns them or, really, how they operate? This sort of question has popped up in the wake of every circus.

The shows, through their press agents, have answered other posers. Do elephants forget? Are the clowns really brokenhearted? And what about triple somersaults? But this is heralding a circus, building interest among potential ticket buyers. And heralding is quite different from history, though one may be as captivating as the other.

The answers that are veiled by the show front of posters and press agents are difficult to reach. By their very nature circuses disguise their own stories in favor of the version the public is to see. The circus is an actor in character, never showing himself; it's like a clown in grease paint. The circus tradition is for minimizing the backyard and front door problems in deference to what appears only in the rings.

John and Alice Durant have been successful in probing their way through this professional shield of circusdom, though not ignoring the shield itself. They have sorted the history from the heralding and put the braggadocio in proper perspective. Their result is "Pictorial History of the American Circus."

Here then is the fast-moving story of circusdom. It is a tale of achievements, battles, victories, heroes and villains that has seldom come to light. As circuses minimized their own stories, they neglected to leave much in the way of records of their action, but the Durants have developed all the sources to find the major events and to turn up the little points of interesting information that decorate the whole story like spangles on a costume.

It is an accurate book, researched at such places as the Hertzberg Collection of the San Antonio Public Library, the theatrical collections of Harvard University and the New York Public Library, the McCaddon Collection at Princeton University, the Museum of the American Circus, the Library of Congress and the New York Historical Society. These are no ordinary archives, but places that come alive with bareback riders, bandwagons and wild animals at the turn of every page.

The Durants have gone on to the most fascinating sources imaginable—the circuses themselves. Ringling Bros. and Barnum & Bailey in its last weeks under canvas, in its winter quarters and in its new form as an indoor circus; Cristiani Bros. Circus, with a family's century of tradition behind it; Hunt Bros., Benson Bros., and more were among the hustling-and-bustling locales where this book had its origins.

A press agent and bill writer of great skill was Charles H. Day, who masterminded Forepaugh's publicity campaigns and did much to build the public's idea of tinseled circuses. Day also was one of the first to realize and seek out the entrancing story of the circuses as differentiated from their performances and performers. That's when Day observed that "he who delves into the early history of the American circus sets himself a hard task; while the theater has historians and records galore, the writer about the early days of arenic amusements has to dig for his data and then search for confirmatory evidence." As it happened, the half-century since Day made his comment has not brought any change in the situation; and some erroneous information has been printed.

Happily, there have been a few exceptions and now among them is the Durants' entrancing way of telling the story. Just as the circus has many avenues of appeal, this book utilizes a combination of text and pictures to convey a feeling for the circus and its lore as no single means could do. The text is a running commentary, not mere captions to identify pictures, but a fact-packed narrative that might stand by itself. But this is not a one-ring show; the Durants have made dramatic use of photographs as well. In no other way can some aspects of the circus and its ornateness be transmitted.

Out of the past then, out of troupers' long-locked trunks and out of the libraries and private collections came the thousands of circus pictures from which to select those hundreds finally chosen. To them were added reproductions of many fine examples of circus artwork and advertising and special pictures photographed by the authors. There are numerous pictures that have not been published before, pictures that will pop the eyes of specialists.

"Pictorial History of the American Circus," however, was not written for the specialists alone. Not any more than circuses are designed for the few. Here is enjoyment for all who have thrilled each spring as their town came alive with circus posters that put color in new places, for those who have waited at cold, dark crossings for overdue circus trains, for those who recall how circus teamsters strapped their raincoats to the harness. It is written for those who experience a special thrill when the spec enters the big top or when a circus band glides from one piece into another. It is written for the old men who saw Barnum and the youngsters who may never see a real circus. There is no limit to the lures that a circus has—in the tents and out—and most everyone falls victim of at least one. It's the same with this book.

Whether one's intrigued by news of the arrival of the first elephant in this country, or by word that George Washington often attended the first American circus, or that heavyweight champion John L. Sullivan once was in circus business, it's all here. Documented here are the strange world of human oddities and the risky ways that decades of daredevils have earned their keep. Names that until now have been only part of familiar circus titles come alive with the personality of the showmen they identify. And it tells the nearly uncharted ways that popularity of the circus has affected American ways of doing everyday things.

In a way this book had to be written and might have been predicted. The authors already have written the *Pictorial History of American Presidents*, *Pictorial History of American Ships*, and, with Dr. Otto Bettman, *Pictorial History of American Sports*.

What else but circuses could be captivating enough to join that trio of colorful subjects?

TOM PARKINSON
Circus Editor
The Billboard

Pictorial History Of The

AMERICAN CIRCUS

John and Alice Durant

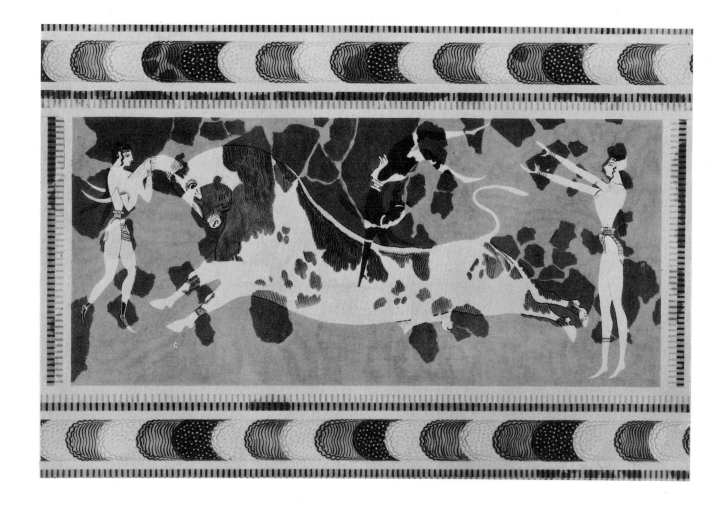

Old World Roots

If the circus can be defined as "an exhibition of skill and daring in an arena or an enclosed space," then the circus is almost as old as humanity itself. This was brought to light by Sir Arthur Evans, excavator of Cnossus on the Island of Crete, who proved that circus-like feats were performed before crowds some 2,400 years before Christ.

A wall painting found by Sir Arthur in a house at Cnossus supports his claim (the restored fresco is shown above). The ancient stunt in which trained Cretian girls and youths took part was that of Bull Leaping and it must have required a tremendous amount of courage and skill, for it was a spectacular and dangerous performance.

Bull Leaping was staged circus-fashion in an arena before a crowd of onlookers who sat in elevated seats. In the arena stood the leapers, scantily clad and unarmed, waiting to meet the challenge of a wild bull. As the animal charged with head lowered the nearest leaper would grasp its horns with both hands and then in an amazing display of agility would swing upwards and turn a complete somersault over the bull's back. Alighting, he would quickly turn about and catch the next leaper. One after another (as the above fresco shows) they would thus perform in a continuous sequence of dodging, leaping and catching. In more than 4,000 years few circus acts have ever bettered the first one.

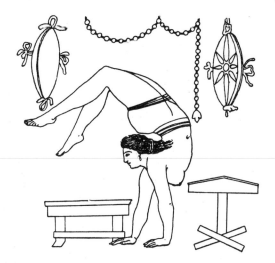

Meanwhile along the Nile Egyptians were being entertained by troupes of acrobats, tumblers, jugglers, and musicians who wandered about the country and put on their acts for a few tossed coins. This was no circus but the elements were there—the roaming companies of skilled performers, the day-to-day venturesome existence. Wall paintings (above and below) indicate the type of acts that pleased the Egyptians. Below: A troupe of acrobats. (In the center young men swing girls in an arc while next to them a human pyramid is being formed.)

The pictures in the right column are of Grecian origin and of a later date. During the Hellenic period itinerant bands moved about giving performances that were similar to those of Egypt. A breathtaker was the girl sword dancer (center) who, "after swords had been fixed with the points upward, immediately leaped headforemost into it through the midst of the points, and then out again with marvelous agility."

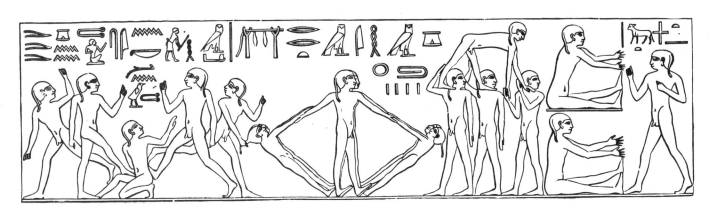

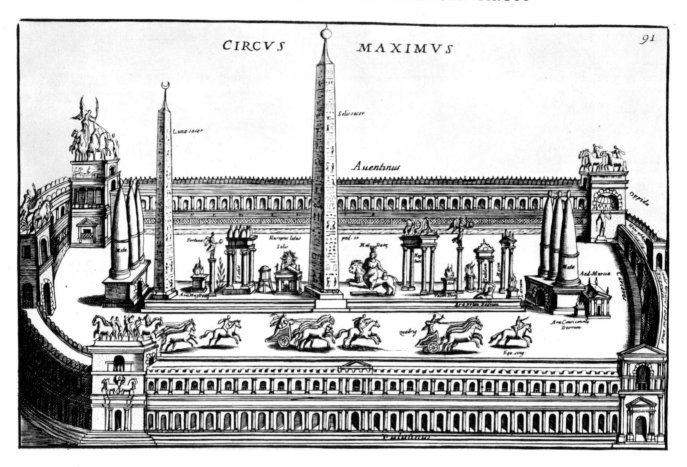

More like the modern circus (but still far removed from it) were the spectacular and bloody shows staged by the Romans in their Circus Maximus, an enormous, 625-yard long structure with seats for more than 150,000 people. Completed in 329 B.C., it was primarily a course for chariot races (above). But often it was the scene of wholesale slaughter, of men against wild beasts (as depicted on the opposite page), animals fighting animals, and men fighting men to the death. Some of the milder events included gymnastic exhibitions (left), rope dancing (opposite page, bottom) and equestrian performances in which riders leaped from one horse to another as they galloped around the track. Thus the Roman circus was in many respects like our own: the parade which always preceded the show, the acrobats, rope walkers, trick riders and chariot races. The flavor of the circus was there, too—the color and noise, the continuous action, the applauding crowds and the overall grand spectacle on a magnificent scale. This was the beginning of the circus as we know it.

As Rome increased in power the character of the circus changed until at length it succumbed almost entirely to spectacles of bloodshed and brutality. The slaughter of animals and humans (long before the Christian era) grew beyond belief. In 55 B.C., for instance, 500 lions, 18 elephants and 410 leopards were killed by archers and javelin throwers in five days. Men were also killed in wholesale lots, deserters from the various wars who were trampled to death by elephants in full view of thousands.

Another kind of arena, the amphitheatre, developed from the Roman taste for bloodshed. Smaller than the circus and bowl-shaped, it gave spectators a closer view. Of the many that were built the largest was the Flavian Amphitheatre, now known as the Coliseum. In this arena events were staged that surpassed in brutality anything the world has ever seen. Favored by the crowd were the games of death.

Turn the page for a view of Jean Leon Gerome's painting "The Gladiators," which shows the crowd ruling "thumbs down" (death) to the conquered.

5

As time passed and the Roman Empire disintegrated so did its circuses and amphitheatres, many of which were scattered throughout the provinces. For more than a thousand years there was no circus, at least no organized one such as the Romans had developed on the grand scale. But the circus did not go into complete eclipse during the Dark Ages. The tradition was kept alive by small groups of performers who traveled about Europe as the Egyptians and Greeks had done before them.

Among them were bands of jugglers and musicians (as above, from a ninth-century drawing), acrobats, rope dancers, contortionists, sword swallowers, conjurers and animal trainers, such as the one shown below whose trick horse beats a tambour with hind and forelegs. Many of these performers were mountebanks (i.e., sellers of medicinal cure-alls and charms) who, like the snake oil medicine men of the last century, would take over a village square, do their stunts and make their spiel.

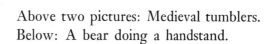

Above: "Tutored Bear" (fourteenth century).
Below: A mountebank and his dancing dog.

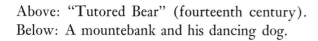

Above two pictures: Medieval tumblers.
Below: A bear doing a handstand.

Typical of the Middle Ages is the above scene of strolling musicians and their trained bear.

More formal and elaborate entertainment is shown below: A tournament (left); court mummers (right).

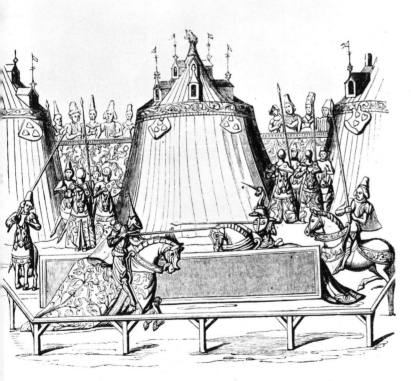

Above: Trainer Banks and his educated horse, Maroccus (1595). The marvel of his age, Maroccus could read dice, dance, count and distinguish colors.

Below: Seventeenth-century rope walkers in the fencing court at Nuremberg stage a mass exhibition. Note the elaborate rigging and lofty center poles.

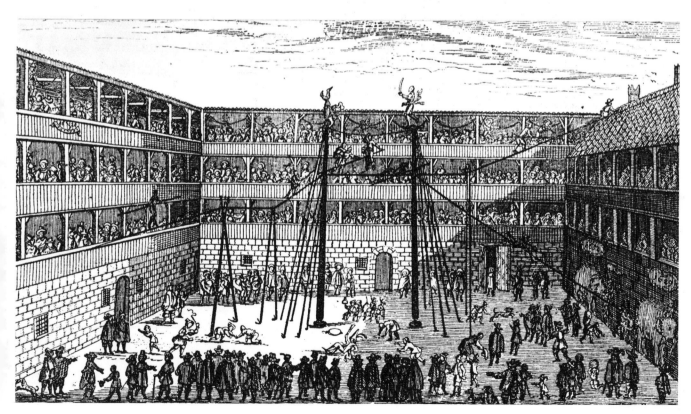

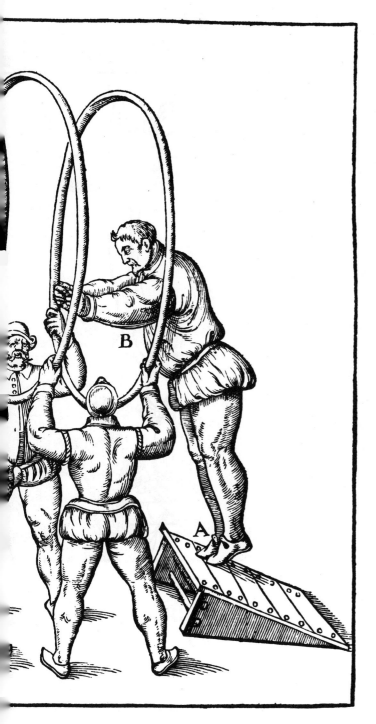

The circus stunt of leaping was developed to a high degree in sixteenth-century Europe, as evidenced by these illustrations. They originally appeared in a French text book on the subject (now extremely rare) which was written by Archange Tuccaro in 1599.

In eighteenth-century England the character of the circus was maintained in its fairs.

Above: Hogarth's engraving of the Southwark Fair (1733). Below: Various performers of that period.

The boisterous English fairs of Hogarth's time were not unlike the carnivals of today—a combination of circus, side show, menagerie, bazaar, waxworks and games of chance.

The above two scenes of England's Bartholomew Fair (dated 1721) show the booths of Lee and Harper, which featured a beheading, and of Faux, the Conjurer.

Below, left: "A Posture Master" (contortionist).

Below: Eighteenth-century leapers.

PHILIP ASTLEY, FATHER
OF THE MODERN CIRCUS

Philip Astley (above) is revered as the founder of the circus because he developed the riding ring which is the basic element of the modern circus.

Trick riding was nothing new in England when Astley established his first circus there in 1768. A notable equestrian was Thomas Johnson, the "Irish Tartar," (below) who thrilled crowds as early as 1758 by riding on one, two and three horses.

Astley himself was a superb rider, an art he learned while serving in the 15th Dragoons as a "rough rider, teacher and horsebreaker." A handsome six-footer with the rough-hewn manners of a sergeant-major, Astley quit the army in 1766 at the age of 24, got married and set up a little open air equestrian show in a field near Westminster Bridge. Out of his profits he built an encircling fence, a house over the entrance and stands with a penthouse room. (Above: Astley's Riding School in 1770.) Soon he added several acts to support his own— a rope walker, a clown, strong man, acrobats, an educated horse and a band (consisting of two pipers and a drum). Thus Astley and his troupe, performing in a ring and offering a variety of circus acts gave birth to the first true circus.

Fame and wealth came to Astley. Talent sought him out, knocked on his circus doors. One of his proteges who reached the heights was Andrew Ducrow, the foremost rider of his time (right).

Par Permission du ROI, & de Monseigneur le Lieuter int-Général de Police.

EXERCICES

S U R P R E N A N S

DES SIEURS

ASTLEY,

RUE ET FAUXBOURG DU TEMPLE,

Aujuourd'hui MERCREDI 27 Décembre 1786.

A good manager and showman, Astley made several trips to Paris during the 1780's and performed there in his own amphitheatre. On one trip a rival showman named Nicolai, taking advantage of a city law which prohibited two performances from being held at the same time on permanent stages, got out an injunction against Astley to prevent his appearance. The resourceful Britisher thwarted Nicolai by constructing a horse-supported stage (above) and the Astley show played before bigger crowds than ever.

A more friendly rival of Astley's was the Parisian showman, Antoine Franconi (left), founder of the *Cirque Olympic* and sire of circus performers. The Franconis became one of the first circus dynasties.

Among the acts featured by Astley (and billed in a large painting at the entrance of his London open air circus) was "The Egyptian Pyramids—An Amusing Performance Of Men Piled Upon Men."

Like most circus men who followed him, Astley had his ups and downs. In 1794 his roofed-over London amphitheatre burned to the ground. He re-opened the following year but the "New Astley's" was destroyed by fire in 1803. In this conflagration (shown below) Astley's aged mother-in-law fell through a window while fighting the flames and was burned to death. Several valuable horses were lost. Again Astley rebuilt, ending his days without further disaster. He died in 1814 at the age of 72.

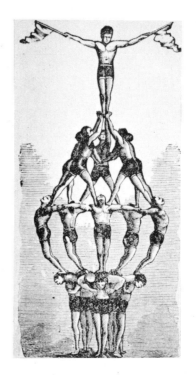

 # Early American Circus

More than a century before the *Mayflower* reached these shores the Aztecs of Mexico were applauding circus acts in the halls of Montezuma and viewing a zoo housed in buildings in which snakes, birds, jaguars and ocelots were kept behind wooden bars. As demonstrated in the above illustration, the "Risley Act" (balancing with the feet while lying on the back) was performed by the Aztecs. (Note the musicians and the three hunch-backed dwarfs in the foreground who were apparently carried for the amusement of their chiefs.)

The Romans would have appreciated one form of Aztec entertainment—the combats which were held in the Great Plaza *Tenochtitlan*, in the center of what is now Mexico City. On a huge elevated circular stone before great crowds two men would have at each other, one a warrior armed with a sharp obsidian sword, the other a captive tethered to a post. His only weapon was a wooden club. It is needless to add which man always won.

The Aztecs did not develop a circus, of course, but they did perform feats of skill that were similar to the circus acts of Rome and Europe.

The forerunner of the circus in this country was perhaps the lone trapper of pioneer days who came out of the woods with a tame bear in tow and showed it on village squares and in frontier taverns for a scattering of coins and a few slugs of rum. These crude animal trainers were encouraged by innkeepers, for they brought business to the bar, as did the occasional sailor who strolled into a taproom with a pet monkey on his shoulders.

Later on came larger animals, brought here from foreign ports by New England skippers with an eye for profit. Boston led the way in animal importation. A lion was shown there in 1716 ("the like never before seen in America"), a camel five years later and the first polar bear in 1733.

To Philadelphia, however, goes the honor of introducing the first circus troupe of record. In 1724 a small company which included a clown gave exhibitions in rope walking and sword dancing in an open arena on the outskirts of the city.

New York got its first look at a circus act in 1753 when Anthony J. Dugee, a slack-rope walker, performed there with his wife, a "Female Sampson."

Mr. POOL,

The firſt American that ever Exhibited the following FEATS OF

HORSEMANSHIP

On the Continent,

Intends Performing this Afternoon, on the Hill near the Jews Burial Ground, if the weather permits, if not, on the firſt fair day afterwards, except Sunday. Mr. POOL has erected a Menage, at a very confiderable expence, with feats raifed from the ground, for the convenient accommodation of thofe Ladies and Gentlemen who may pleafe to honour him with their company.

A CLOWN will entertain the Ladies and Gentlemen between the Feats.

1. MOUNTS a fingle Horfe in full fpeed, ftanding on the top of the faddle, and in that pofition carries a glafs of wine in his hand, drinks it off, and falls to his feat on the faddle.
2. Mounts a fingle Horfe in half fpeed, ftanding on the faddle, throws up an Orange, and catches it on the point of a fork.
3. Mounts two Horfes in full fpeed, ftanding on the faddles, and fires a piftol.
4. Mounts two Horfes in full fpeed, with a foot in the ftirrup of each faddle, from thence to the ground, and from thence to the tops of the faddles at the fame fpeed.
5. Mounts two Horfes in full fpeed, ftanding on the faddles, and in that pofition leaps a bar.
6. Mounts a fingle Horfe in full fpeed, fires a piftol, falls backward, with his head to the ground, hanging by his right leg, and rifes again to his feat on the faddle.
7. Mounts three Horfes in full fpeed, ftanding on the faddles, and in that pofition leaps a bar.

After which Mr. POOL will introduce a very extraordinary Horfe, who, at the word of command, will lay himfelf down and groan, apparently through extreme ficknefs and pain; after which he will rife and fit up like a lady's lap-dog, then rife to his feet and make his Manners to the Ladies and Gentlemen.

The entertainment will conclude with the noted fcene, THE TAYLOR RIDING TO BRENTFORD.

*** Every time of Performance there will be new Feats.—Mr. POOL flatters himfelf the Ladies and Gentlemen who may be pleafed to honour him with their Company, will have no reafon to go away diffatisfied;—he even hopes to merit their approbation.

The doors will be opened at Three o'Clock, and the Performance will begin at Four in the afternoon precifely.

TICKETS to be had at Mr. CHILDS's Printing-Office, near the Coffee-Houfe; Mrs. DELAMATER's, next Door to the Play-Houfe; and at the PLACE of PERFORMANCE. Price for the Firſt Seats FOUR SHILLINGS—for the Second, THREE SHILLINGS.

‡§‡ Mr. POOL befeeches the Ladies and Gentlemen who honour him with their Prefence, to bring no dogs with them to the Place of Performance.

‖+‖ The Exhibitions will be on TUESDAYS and FRIDAYS.

New York, September 21, 1786.

Broadly speaking, the strolling animal men of the eighteenth century played the hamlets and towns of rural America (as shown in these cuts) while the equestrians, rope walkers and acrobats performed only in the larger cities.

The first native American equestrian was a Mr. Pool who gave performances in his Philadelphia riding school in 1785 and the following year took his act to New York (note handbill, right). Pool worked with an educated horse and a clown.

The first complete circus performance in America was given by John Bill Ricketts, an English equestrian, in his newly built amphitheatre in Philadelphia on April 3, 1793. President George Washington, an enthusiastic circus fan, attended Ricketts' show on April 22 and 24 in company with his lady, Martha.

Ricketts advertised his show as a circus and it was held in a building constructed for that purpose. For this reason and because his company endured and kept its identity while playing New York, Albany, and several New England cities, Ricketts' circus is recognized as the first one in America.

America had never seen a rider like John Bill Ricketts. Some of his stunts would get by in any circus today. One of them, as described in a handbill printed in 1793, was his leap "over a riband suspended 12 feet high and at the same time through a cane held in both hands with the horse in full gallop." Ricketts' well-rounded circus offered a rope walker, a clown, several equestrians and his horse, Cornplanter, which leaped over the back of another horse (right).

Ricketts had such remarkable success that he was able to build an amphitheatre in New York and a second and larger one in Philadelphia (below). But at the zenith of his career luck turned against him. In 1799 both places burned down. Penniless, Ricketts sailed for England and was lost at sea.

Captain Jacob Crowninshield (left), a Salem ship-master, made circus history of a sort on April 13, 1796 when his ship *America* (below) sailed into New York harbor with a three-year-old female elephant, the first ever seen in this country. The strange, new animal was a sensation. The Captain, who had paid $450 for her in Bengal, soon sold her for $10,000 to a Philadelphian named Owen.

The nameless elephant went on the road and toured the eastern seaboard, leaving a trail in the form of handbills and newspaper notices that stretches from South Carolina to upstate New York. (Note handbill, opposite page.) In Cooperstown, New York, she was exhibited in October, 1813, and advertised as "an elephant upwards of 8 feet and weighs more than 5,700 pounds . . . the only one in the U.S." The trail ends in York, Pennsylvania, where she was shown in July, 1818.

THE
ELEVANT,

ACCORDING to the account of the celebrated BUFFON, is the moſt reſpectable Animal in the world. In ſize he ſurpaſſes all other terreſtrial creatures; and by his intelligence, as near an approach to man, as matter can approach ſpirit. A ſufficient proof that there too much ſaid of the knowledge of this animal is, that the Proprietor having been abſent n weeks, the moment he arrived at the door of his apartment, and ſpoke to the keeper, the al's knowledge was beyond any doubt confirmed by the cries he uttered forth, till his Friend within reach of his trunk, with which he careſſed him, to the aſtoniſhment of all thoſe who im. This moſt curious and ſurpriſing animal is juſt arrived in this town, from Philadel- where he will ſtay but a few days.——— He is only four years old, and weighs about 3000 t, but will not have come to his full growth till he ſhall be between 30 and 40 years old. eaſures from the end of his trunk to the tip of his tail 15 feet 8 inches, round the body 10 inches; round his head 7 feet 2 inches, round his leg above the knee 3 feet 3 inches, his ankle 2 feet 2 inches. He eats 130 weight a day, and drinks all kinds of ſpirituous s; ſome days he has drank 30 bottles of porter, drawing the corks with his trunk. He ame that he travels looſe, and has never attempted to hurt any one. He appeared on ge, at the New Theatre in Philadelphia, to the great ſatisfaction of a reſpectable audience. reſpectable and convenient place is fitted up adjoining the Store of Mr. Bartlet, Market- , for the reception of thoſe ladies and gentlemen who may be pleaſed to view the greateſt l curioſity ever preſented to the curious, which is to be ſeen from ſunriſe till ſundown, day in the week.
 The Elephant having deſtroyed many papers of conſequence, it is recommended to not to come near him with ſuch papers.

mittance ONE QUARTER OF A DOLLAR——Children ONE EIGHTH OF A DOL.

NEWBURYPORT, Sept. 19, 1797.

More important in circus history was Old Bet, the second elephant to reach these shores. Hachaliah Bailey of Somers, New York, bought her for $1,000 in 1815 and did so well showing her around the countryside that he added other animals to his exhibit. Several of Bailey's neighbors soon followed his example and went into the touring menagerie business. Among them were Aron Turner, John J. June, Lewis B. Titus, Caleb S. Angevine and the Howes and Crane families, all of whom dwelt within a day's buggy ride of each other in an area some fifty miles north of New York City. The section has come to be known as the Cradle of the American Circus.

Old Bet was shot down in Maine by an irate farmer. Bailey erected a statue to her memory (right) in front of his Elephant Hotel in Somers.

One of the first great American showmen was Rufus Welch (below), born in upstate New York in 1801. A venturesome pioneer, Welch toured the West Indies with his own circus in 1829, went to Africa in the 1830's and returned with the largest herd of animals ever brought here.

In the early 1820's there were thirty or more rolling animal shows touring the eastern United States from Maine to Alabama and west to the Appalachians. They were primitive affairs of two or three wagons (as indicated above) and most of them owed their origin to the farmers-turned-showmen of Somers and vicinity.

One menagerie, however, which was independent of the Somers group but which was later absorbed by it, was the Zoological Institute (opposite page). It began as a tiny road show before 1820 but grew in size to become the largest and most valuable menagerie in the country. Quartered for many years in a permanent building on the Bowery in New York, the Institute held a virtual monopoly in the menagerie business, leasing its animals to various caravans on its own terms.

The menagerie and the equestrian circus developed side by side as separate types of entertainment, each independent of the other. The fusion of the two was gradual. At first a few trick animals were introduced into the equestrian circus and given a very minor role in the performance. Later a cage or two of wild animals were used as an added attraction. A rival showman noting the box-office value would answer with more and rarer animals. In this way, through rivalry, the combination of the circus and menagerie came into being.

They were hardy men who traveled the miserable roads of back country America with the early rolling shows. They moved in wagons with a few head of stock and showed in enclosures made by stretching canvas side walls around posts and trees. If it rained there was no performance unless a vacant hall or theater could be found. At best these shows were haphazard affairs. No regular salaries were paid; there was no closely planned itinerary and every man was expected to perform several jobs.

The shows were ballyhooed by an advance agent and a clown. First came the agent on horseback a week or so ahead of the show. He tacked up handbills in taverns and stores and talked up the show, sometimes ringing a bell to attract attention. On the day of arrival the clown led the show into town by a couple of hours. He would draw a crowd on the village green with his tumbling antics and wisecracks. Then he would proclaim the wonders of the show and announce the starting time.

Joe Pentland, a favorite of the pre-Civil War days,   was one of the first clowns to rate top billing.

Moving at night over country roads that were often a foot deep in mud, a wagon train could make only two or three miles an hour. A good jump between towns was ten or fifteen miles. Ahead of the train rode the hostler whose job it was to find the shortest route and "rail" the road at every fork and crossroad so that the wagons would not make a wrong turn. This he did by taking a rail from a farmer's fence and placing it across the road that was to be avoided.

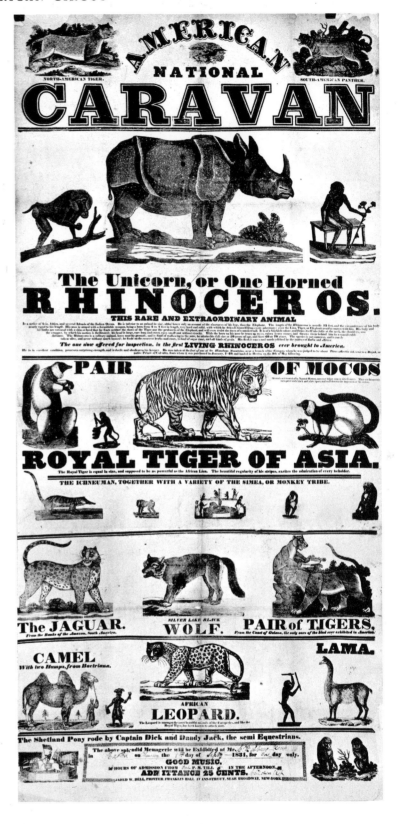

Left: "The Bedouin Arabs," a circus act of 1838.
Above: An 1831 poster. In this decade the circus
and menagerie began to merge into one attraction.

Van - Amburgh. 1811

America's first animal trainer of note was Isaac A. Van Amburgh (1811-65) who astounded the country by entering a cage of wild animals on the stage of the Richmond Hill Theatre, New York, in 1833. The performance, as described in lurid terms by his biographer, O. J. Ferguson, follows:

"He was attired in a dress designed to convey an impression to the beasts of the field that man, in accordance with the decree of God, was and should be the monarch of the Universe. The daring pioneer approached the door of the den with a firm step and unaverted eye. A murmur of alarm and horror involuntarily escaped the audience. If Van Amburgh had possessed a nerve like ten thousand, nay, ten million men, he would have quailed and fallen a victim to the fury of the animals. But the effect of his power was instantaneous. The Lion halted and stood transfixed. The Tiger crouched. The Panther with a suppressed growl of rage sprang back, while the Leopard receded gradually from its master. The spectators were overwhelmed with wonder . . . Then came the most effective tableaux of all. Van Amburgh with his strong will bade them come to him while he reclined in the back of the cage—the proud King of animal creation.

"Van Amburgh's fame spread through civilization and is now contemporaneous and extensive with the Universe itself."

THE CAVALCADE.

THE Animals will be accompanied by one of the most costly and superbly attired pageants ever witnessed. This immense and imposing Cavalcade being composed of One Hundred Iron Grey Horses, besides the colossal team of the Chariot, will make its appearance in each town advertised for exhibition at about 11 o'clock, A. M., and make a Grand Procession through all the principal streets, at which time the public will have an opportunity of beholding the magnitude and splendor of the "Van Amburgh" Caravan. It will be preceded by a magnificent

ROMAN CHARIOT,

OR, IMPERIAL STATE CARRIAGE AND THRONE,

DRAWN BY THE LARGEST TEAM IN THE WORLD !!.

While Van Amburgh's fame may not have been quite that extensive he did become internationally known and gave command performances before Queen Victoria. The originator of several stunts, he made a lion and a lamb lie down together and later brought a child into the den "thus completing the picture of the triumph of faith over the savage beast." Van Amburgh earned up to $400 a week and saved enough money to start his own show.

His great bandwagon ("the largest ever seen on the continent") as displayed in 1846 (above), was over twenty feet long and seventeen feet high to the top of the canopy which could be lowered for passing under bridges. Following it in the Grand Procession came the "Carriages, Cages and Performing Caverns, thirty in number and all entirely new."

Van Amburgh died in 1865, a wealthy man. His name, however, was used as a circus title until 1908.

33

THE GOOD SHIP "TASSO"

Among the gold-seekers who crowded the bark *Tasso* when it arrived in San Francisco on October 12, 1849 was a small company of troupers headed by Joseph A. Rowe, an equestrian. Twenty years before at the age of ten he had run off with a circus playing Kingston, North Carolina, and that was the last his home town ever saw of him.

The lad grew up in the circus, joined several shows and trouped the West Indies and South America. Rowe was playing Lima, Peru, with his own show when he decided to try California where gold had recently been discovered and the rush was on. California saw its first circus on October 29, 1849, in a theater on Kearney Street, San Francisco.

SAN FRANCISCO IN 1849.

Rowe's Olympic Circus opened to an audience of about 1,500 and was greeted with "thunders of applause," according to the newspaper *Alta California*, which further stated that "Mr. Rowe's circus entertainments will relieve the tedium of many a long winter evening." Featured were Mrs. Rowe ("a female equestrian of pleasing merit"), a riding clown, two rope dancers, Rowe's trained horse, Adonis ("a perfectly tutored animal") and Rowe as a trick rider. Admission was $3, box seats $5. (These were gold rush prices. Admission to top eastern shows at the time was 50 cents. Rowe's clown, Folley, quit the show because he couldn't live on his $1,200 a month salary.)

Rowe played San Francisco for a year, later went to Australia and came back with $100,000. He retired in 1854 but reopened two years later and toured the mining districts in the interior. By this time the boom was over. Admission sank to 50 cents; a good day's take was $250.

JOSEPH A. ROWE

MISS MARY ANN WHITTAKER

With a bandwagon (below) and a company of thirty-three Rowe tried the mining towns again in 1857 but had a disastrous season. Still worse was his trip to Australia a year later. The show folded and Rowe held assorted jobs: Menagerie manager, ringmaster, advance agent, engraver and horse trainer. His death on November 3, 1887 was unnoticed.

The year Rowe opened in California, R. Sands & Co. was papering the east with the above poster.

As far as is known this is the first poster to be printed in full color from hand-cut wood blocks.

"The Apollo on Horseback" was one of the many names given to Levi J. North (above), a slim-bodied, handsome rider of consummate grace. He stood only five and a half feet and wore his sandy hair long like most performers of his day. England first saw the American-born perfectionist at Astley's in 1838 when he defeated acrobat James Price in a man-to-man springboard vaulting contest.

But it was North's riding that put his name above all others. In 1839 he turned a full feet-to-feet somersault on the back of a running horse—the first one ever, according to most historians. The "North Star" brightened the ring for nearly forty years, always a star in his own and other circuses. North, age 52, and still a star, ended his riding career in 1866 with Lent's New York Circus.

The name Howes stands high in circus achievement. First of the line was Nathan B. Howes (1796-1878) of Brewster, New York, a town near Somers in the Cradle of the American Circus. With his partner, Aron Turner, Howes put a show together in the 1830's that was the first to go out under a full top canvas—a milestone in circus history.

Nathan's brother Seth (right), younger by fifteen years, started his career at twenty-one as assistant to his brother, later managed and bought into various shows. In 1857 in partnership with Joseph C. Cushing, he embarked for England with the greatest show yet seen, Howes and Cushing's. It stayed abroad for seven years, delighted English audiences at London's Alhambra (above) and performed before Queen Victoria. Seth B. Howes' Great European and Great London circuses (1864-72) brought millions to its owner. He was the foremost showman of his time.

Jean François Gravelet, the great French funambulist (rope walker) who had light yellow hair and was known to the world as Blondin, is shown above making his first ascent at the Crystal Palace in London, June, 1861 (from the *Illustrated Times*).

Blondin had previously thrilled American crowds by walking across the Niagara gorge several times. His act inspired the cartoon (opposite page) which shows an uncertain Lincoln trying to cope with the slavery question (from *Vanity Fair*, June 9, 1860).

SHAKY

DARING TRANSIT ON THE PERILOUS RAIL, - - - - Mr. Abraham Blondin De Lave Lincoln.

DAN RICE.
"The King of American Clowns."

Dan Rice (1823-1900), America's first great clown and one of the most beloved figures of the last century, was a sharp-tongued wit with a sonorous voice who looked like Uncle Sam. For years Dan dominated every show he worked, made and lost fortunes and had a following that no other performer of his time could match. He commanded the largest salary ever paid a circus clown ($1,000 a week)—more than Lincoln earned as President. Circus owners fought for his services. Dan jumped from one show to another but for many seasons ran his own outfit.

Born Daniel McLaren in New York City, he became a professional jockey in his teens and rode as Dan Rice, a name given him by his father in honor of the Irish clown of that name. A traveling puppet show picked him up in 1840 and paid him $4 a week to exhibit his trained pig, Lord Byron. Dan soon became a versatile performer—a slack wire artist, strong man, jig dancer and singer of comic songs. In 1844 he gave his first circus performance.

DAN RICE'S GREAT SHOW

Dan was only twenty-one when he joined Spalding's North American Circus but he was a hit from the start. He drew so well that owner Spalding organized Dan Rice's Circus in 1848 and let the clown manage it. (This was the first of many shows that bore the Rice name.) In the following years Dan played to packed houses from New Orleans to New England. A born wag and the possessor of a fine voice, he magnetized his audiences. He would open a show alone, exchange quips with the crowd and the ringmaster, spout doggerel, dance jigs and offer a variety of songs, many of which he had composed. (His most popular song: "Root Hog or Die.")

His humor was original and earthy, sharp or gentle. The chin-whiskered clown was the embodiment of rustic America—the hayseed with the bright retort.

Dan was not all clown. He could fight, and did, whenever there was trouble with the towners. Circus men who worked with him put him at the top as a battler. Dan never lost a fight with his fists. His weakness was the bottle. Dan drank himself out of jobs, ran out on contracts and began to slide downhill. Toward the end he became a temperance lecturer. He died broke in Long Branch, New Jersey, aged 77. The *New York Times* obituary gave the once great clown only two paragraphs.

"WILL S. HAYS"

The *Will S. Hays* (above), a 340-ton steamer built in 1865, was one of several river boats that plied the Mississippi with Dan Rice's "Brilliant Combination of Arenic Attractions" on board. Dan played the southern river towns, always setting up on land. In the North his shows moved by wagon.

Below: Rice's show on the lot at Jamestown, New York, on July 9, 1864, showing the Big Top (number 4) and side show (in center of photo).

Above: Dan Rice as he looked in the 1860's at the zenith of his career.

Opposite page: a handbill announcing his appearance at the Walnut Street Theatre, Philadelphia.

WALNUT STREET THEATRE
NINTH AND WALNUT STS., PHILADELPHIA.

SOLE LESSEE,   - - - -   MRS. M. A. GARRETTSON
STAGE MANAGER,   - - - -   MR. G. VINING BOWERS
BUSINESS AGENT,   - - - -   MR. J. T. DONNELLY

Doors open at quarter to 7.   The Curtain will rise at quarter past 7

Re-Engagement, and Positively Last Night but Three of

DAN RICE
THE GREATEST LIVING HUMORIST,
Together with his MODEL TROUPE of EQUESTRIANS.

WEDNESDAY, MARCH 12th, 1862

Come Boys and have some Fun.   *A Ride on Dan. Rice's Mules.*

TWO Performances
THIS DAY!

In the AFTERNOON, ESPECIALLY for FAMILY PARTIES, commencing at half-past 2 o'clk.

Great Success of MADAM TOURNAIRE
And her Wonderful Horse, KOLE.

Madam Tournaire in Two Acts.

This marble bust of Dan Rice was chiseled in 1863 by Leonard Welles Volk, a noted sculptor of the last century. It remained in the Rice family until 1952 when it was given to the Harry Hertzberg Circus Collection in the Public Library at San Antonio, Texas, by Rice's grandson, James Connolly.

The black-face, or Negro impersonator, enjoyed his first big success in the circus. Cavorting about the ring, singing songs and sassing the ringmaster, these burnt-cork clowns were featured in many of the early shows both here and abroad.

Such a comic was Joe Sweeney, the "Father of the Banjoe," who rated top billing in Sand's American Circus when it played in London in 1842 (below). From these early black-face routines of the circus developed the stylized minstrel show.

VIEW OF THE FLOATING PALACE IN THE GULF OF MEXICO,

IN HER PASSAGE FROM MOBILE TO THE BALISE

IN THE MEMORABLE STORM OF THE 28 OF JANUARY 1853, IN WHICH THE GUARDS OF HER CONSORT THE NORTH RIVER, WHICH HAD HER IN TOW, WERE CUT AWAY TO ESCAPE SHIPWRECK.

Gilbert R. "Doc" Spalding (left) was running a drugstore near Albany, New York, in 1843 when he took over a busted circus and went into show business. Spalding invented the quarter poles (used to take up slack between the center and side poles) and the stringer and jack type of 11-tier seats, thereby setting the standard. He used oil for illumination instead of the customary cluster of candles, and was the first to move a show on rails (1858). He is most remembered, however, for his *Floating Palace*, a magnificent showboat.

The above lithograph shows the *Floating Palace* and her towing steamboat *North River* in the throes of a storm off Mobile in 1853, the second season of the showboat's fourteen-year career.

The *Floating Palace*, built at a cost of $42,000 in Cincinnati, was an amphitheatre constructed on a flat-bottomed barge which drew four feet. It had a standard sized 42-foot circus ring, a seating capacity of 2,400 and was gorgeously decorated with velvet hangings, thick carpets, mirrors and carved woodwork. It was lighted by over 200 gas jets and heated by steam, the apparatus for which was on the towboat. Also on the towboat was the menagerie.

Spalding & Rogers *Floating Palace* opened in Pittsburgh in March, 1852, and was an immediate success. An all-year around attraction, the show annually toured the Ohio and Mississippi, making a long stand in New Orleans during the winter. The *Palace* was idle during the Civil War. In the spring of 1865 she burned to the waterline.

The Great Barnum

Phineas Taylor Barnum, who is caricatured on the opposite page as an attention-seeker like the strutting birds about him, was the first showman to make widespread use of the press to advertise himself and his wares. As a result, and because of his vivid imagination and promotional genius, he was one of the most talked about men in America during the last century. His fame endures. In 1940, nearly fifty years after his death, Professor William Lyons Phelps of Yale called him "The greatest showman who ever lived . . . the greatest psychologist who ever lived . . . the Shakespeare of advertising."

Phineas was born in Bethel, Connecticut, on July 5, 1810 (above, his birthplace). The name "Phineas" means "mouth of brass" and a more fitting name could not have been chosen for the greatest self-advertiser in history.

In 1836 he joined Aron Turner's circus as ticket seller. On tour in Maryland Phineas learned his first lesson in the value of publicity, although it nearly cost him his life.

Turner, a practical joker, told an Annapolis mob that Barnum was a wanted murderer. They seized him (below) and might have killed him had not Turner intervened. Later Turner chuckled, "It's all for our good. The notoriety will fill our tent."

51

THE AMERICAN MUSEUM
BROADWAY, N. Y.
1850.

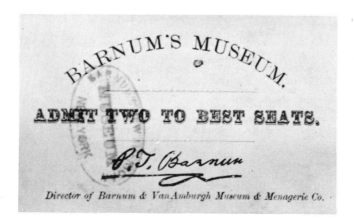

BARNUM'S MUSEUM.

ADMIT TWO TO BEST SEATS.

P. T. Barnum

Director of Barnum & Van Amburgh Museum & Menagerie Co.

After his first circus venture Barnum scratched out a bare living for the next several years. At thirty-one he was penniless, living with his wife and two daughters in New York where, on Broadway and Ann Street, stood Scudder's American Museum. When Barnum heard that the Museum was for sale (for $15,000) he determined to buy it. "What with?" he was asked. "With brass," replied Barnum, "for gold and silver I have none." With brass and credit he took over the Museum and opened it under his name on New Year's Day, 1842.

The five-story building was jammed with a permanent collection of musty curiosities when Barnum took the helm. He at once realized that the Museum must be brought to life with an ever-changing variety of exhibits and that a vigorous publicity campaign must be launched to make people aware of it. The wheels started to roll in the summer of 1842 when Barnum acquired a hideous exhibit (a dead monkey's head and torso sewn to a fish's body) which he billed as the "Fejee Mermaid" (right). He planted stories in newspapers supposedly written by scientists attesting to the authenticity of the mermaid and distributed a pamphlet "proving" that such creatures existed. Thousands rushed to the Museum to see the fake mermaid. At the end of Barnum's first year profits were close to $30,000, about three times the amount taken in the previous year. In addition to the curiosities the Museum had a collection of living wild animals, several panoramas of Biblical scenes, displays of new gadgets and inventions, educated fleas, freaks, and a theater (below).

Since the word "theater" was distasteful to many in those more puritanical times, Barnum named it the Lecture Room and staged what he called "refined amusements and moral dramas."

Barnum made his first fortune by making a world sensation out of a perfectly formed midget named Charles Stratton. (Left, little Charlie with his father, a Bridgeport carpenter.) Barnum took the lad in hand, brought him to New York in 1842 and billed him at the Museum as General Tom Thumb from England, aged eleven. The boy was actually four but had stopped growing at five months. He was only twenty-five inches tall and weighed fifteen pounds. Not until he was fourteen did he increase in size, and then only a few inches. He was bright, good looking, pert and responded readily to Barnum's coaching. (Below, left: Barnum teaches him to play Napoleon.) Tom Thumb's skits, jokes and songs drew thousands to the Museum. A day's average gate was $500, split between Barnum and Tom's parents.

After two years at the Museum and a tour of the eastern seaboard Barnum took Tom to Europe. The day they sailed 80,000 people stormed the Museum and lined the streets to see them off. In England Tom charmed Queen Victoria (below), was thrice received by her. He toured Europe and became the pet of society in France, Spain and Belgium. Tom traveled in style—in a miniature carriage drawn by matched ponies with two small children on the box dressed in sky-blue livery and cocked hats.

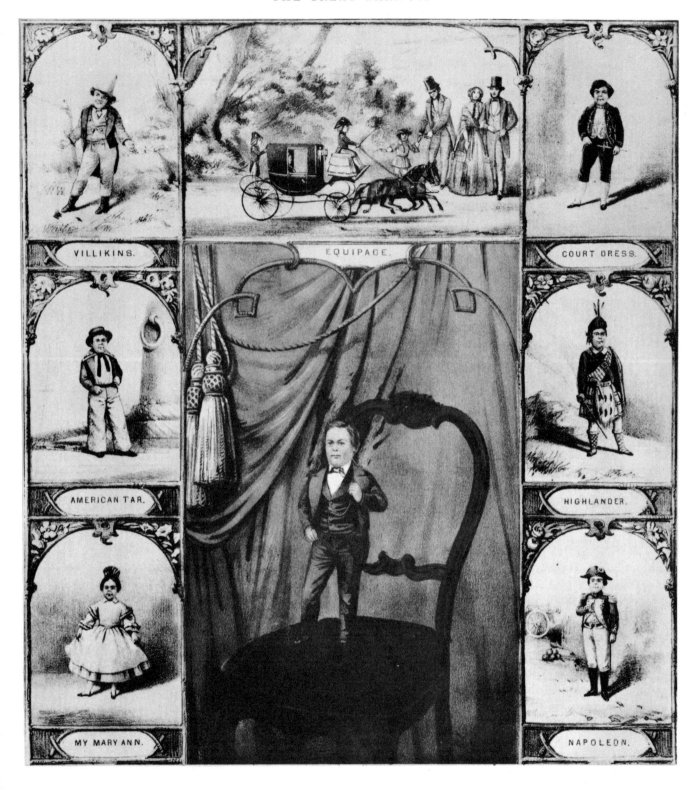

Of the many roles Tom played during his four-year tour abroad, his "Napoleon" was best received (in England). Pacing the floor as Napoleon one day, he was asked by the Duke of Wellington what he was pondering. "The loss of Waterloo," chirped Tom, without smiling.

"The General left America a diffident, unculti-vated little boy," wrote Barnum in his autobiog-raphy. "He came back an educated, accomplished little man . . . "He went abroad poor, and he came home rich." Barnum came home rich, too, and so did Tom's father.

In Lavina Warren Tom found a pretty midget bride. A few years after their marriage (in 1863) a baby girl was supposedly born to them (above, right) and the nation was thrilled. It was a borrowed baby, however—a publicity scheme of Barnum's. In later years Tom, who loved fine wines and rich food, blew up to a portly seventy pounds and sported a goatee (right). The little man lived like a prince. He had a stable of horses, a yacht and a grand mansion. He died at forty-five in 1883.

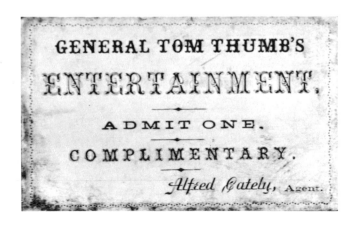

GENERAL TOM THUMB'S
ENTERTAINMENT.
ADMIT ONE.
COMPLIMENTARY.
Alfred Gately, Agent.

A big hearty man standing six feet two inches and weighing over 200 pounds, Barnum had a putty-like nose, curly brown hair, blue eyes and the booming voice of a ringmaster. Although he was often called a faker, or humbug, as this caricature (right) indicates, he was just as often forgiven for his frauds and exaggerations which most people accepted as part of a showman's game. "The public likes to be fooled," grinned the genial Barnum.

In character with his flair for publicity, Barnum built an ornate, showy residence in Bridgeport which was a combination of Turkish, Moorish and Byzantine architecture (below). It stood in the middle of a seventeen-acre park in full view of the railroad tracks so that it "might serve," said Barnum, "as an advertisement of my various enterprises." It could be seen for three miles. Named *Iranistan*, (Oriental villa), the showplace was a hodgepodge of domes, minarets, spires, piazzas and lattices. Its interior was equally ornate. It cost Barnum $200,000 to build and furnish the place. Nearly a thousand guests attended the housewarming on November 14, 1848. Deer and elk roamed the park. Fountains played under transplanted trees. "Why, it's as elegant as a steamboat," murmured one of the guests.

Songstress Jenny Lind was riotously greeted by New Yorkers upon her arrival. On September 11, 1850, she gave her first concert at Castle Garden (below), before 7,000, a capacity crowd.

P.T. BARNUM introducing MADELLE JENNY LIND to OSSIAN E. DODGE

THE "BOSTON VOCALIST,"

and purchaser of the $625 TICKET for the first Concert of the Sweedish Nightingale in Boston.

The idea of engaging Jenny Lind to give a series of concerts in America first came to Barnum when he was in England in 1849. The Swedish soprano had been acclaimed throughout Europe but she was hesitant about signing with Barnum for fear that he would exhibit her as one of his museum freaks. A fat contract, however, changed her mind: She would sing in 150 concerts at $1,000 a performance plus all expenses for her maid, butler and secretary, and an additional $25,000 for her musical director.

Tickets were in such demand at her initial concerts that they were sold by auction. The lucky bidder for the first ticket for Jenny's Boston premier was Ossian E. Dodge (above, with Barnum and Jenny) who paid $625 to sit alone. Jenny conquered America as she had Europe. At the end of her tour, in May 1852, gross receipts amounted to nearly $700,000. To Barnum this meant a net cash profit of about a quarter of a million dollars. But his profit in prestige was worth far more than that.

BARNUM'S MAMMOTH TENT.

A few months before Jenny Lind's arrival, Barnum, who had his fingers in everything, chartered a ship and sent her to India for a cargo of animals for his Museum. His partners were Seth B. Howes and Sherwood Stratton, Tom Thumb's father. In 1851 the three men organized the show, P. T. Barnum's Great Asiatic Caravan, Museum and Menagerie. Their 110-foot long tent was truly a mammoth one compared to most of the little round tops touring the country at that time (below).

The Barnum show featured General Tom Thumb, Mr. Nellis, an armless wonder, Mr. Pierce in a den of lions, ten elephants, wax statues of the Presidents, a "fine military band" and other "wonderful objects of nature and art." There were no ring acts. The show was not advertised as a circus. Admission was twenty-five cents, children half price.

At the end of a four-year profitable tour the partnership was dissolved and Barnum turned his hand to enlarging and improving his Museum.

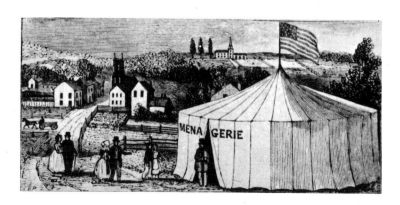

Barnum paraded his elephants in every town. When the show broke up he sold all save one which he put to plowing a field adjoining *Iranistan* in view of the railroad tracks. Daily hundreds of passengers gaped at the strange sight. The attendant publicity, as Barnum planned, increased interest in his Museum.

Barnum was the first showman to exhibit freaks on a large scale and, as this poster reveals, they could be seen in wholesale lots in his American Museum.

Although Barnum made side excursions into various promotions his heart was in the Museum. For years it was New York's most popular place of amusement, a real resort where families brought their lunches and spent the whole day. The doors opened at sunrise so that country visitors arriving in New York at an early hour could see the Museum before going to their hotels. For twenty-five cents they were offered a continuous program which lasted from dawn until 10 o'clock at night. Barnum liked to boast that his Museum daily outdrew the free-of-charge British Museum.

He did little boasting, though, when Dan Rice played a trick on him following a salary dispute between the two. In Dan's strongman act at the Museum a huge hogshead borne by six men was carried on the stage and placed on his back. Dripping water to show that it was full, the hogshead supposedly weighed a ton. One day after the straining men put the cask on Dan he held it aloft with ease, then let out its entire contents—a pailfull of water from a hidden compartment. Dan walked off laughing. Barnum never forgave him for exposing the hoax.

Almost every place Barnum ever owned was completely destroyed by fire. *Iranistan* burned to the ground in 1857, his first Museum in 1865 and his second one three years later. (In this disaster fireman Johnny Denham made a name for himself by killing an escaped tiger with his axe and carrying out of the burning building a fat lady who weighed 400 pounds.) In 1872 Barnum's Hippotheatron on 14th Street, which housed his valuable menagerie, was totally consumed by flames with a loss of $300,000. Again Barnum suffered fiery disaster when in 1887 his circus winter quarters at Bridgeport burned down. The loss on this, his fifth fire, totalled $250,000.

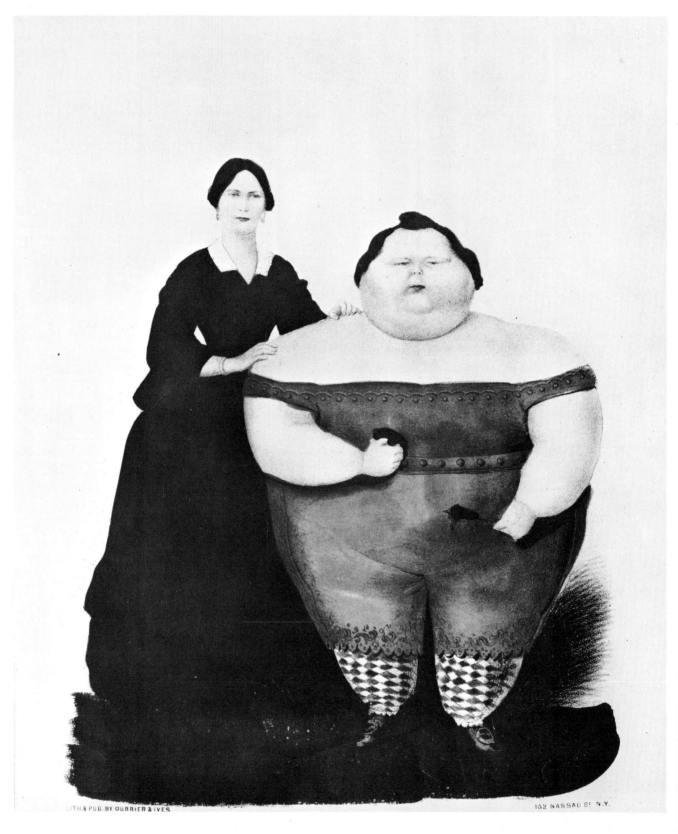

One of Barnum's freaks was this fat boy, shown with his mother. He was billed as: "VANTILE MACK, THE GIANT BABY! Weighs 257 pounds! 7 years old, measures 38 inches around the leg!!"

Madame Josephine Clofullia, the Bearded Lady from Switzerland, was summoned to court after a few appearances at the Museum and charged with being a fraud. (Unknown to anyone, Barnum had secretly instigated the charges as a publicity stunt.) In court Barnum produced three doctors who had examined her. They testified that Madame Clofullia was indeed a lady, as did her husband who had fathered her two children. The case was thrown out of court. Barnum's scheme worked to perfection. Newspapers played up the story and customers stormed the Museum to see the Bearded Lady.

THE CARDIFF GIANT

Only Barnum would have enough brass to make a fake of a fake and advertise it as the real thing. The original fake was the Cardiff Giant, a ten-foot stone man unearthed on October 16, 1869, on the farm of "Stub" Newell at Cardiff, a village near Syracuse, New York (left). A year before it had secretly been buried by Stub and his partner, George Hull. A WONDERFUL DISCOVERY! THE PETRI-FIED GIANT! screamed newspaper headlines a few days after the Giant was dug up. Thousands flocked to the scene to view the monster (below) which many scientists declared to be a genuine petrified man. Barnum rushed to Cardiff, took one look and said, "And they call *me* a humbug!" Nevertheless he offered the owners $60,000 for a three-month lease on the Giant. He was refused (the owners were making a fortune), but not to be outdone Barnum had an exact copy made of plaster and exhibited it in New York as the original Cardiff Giant. When the owners of the real hoax arrived in the city with *their* Giant they tried to get an injunction to prevent the display of Barnum's imitation. Failing in this, they left town and Barnum, supreme, made thousands by showing a fake of a fake.

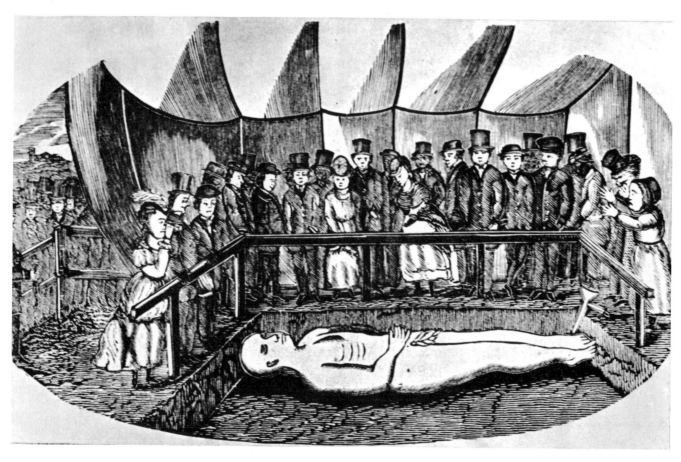

W. C. COUP, CIRCUS MANAGER.

The forerunner of "The Greatest Show On Earth" was conceived by W. C. Coup and Dan Castello, a former clown, who persuaded Barnum to join them in staging a mammoth circus. Barnum agreed to furnish his name and money to the project, the other two their experience and energy.

The show opened in Brooklyn on April 10, 1871, under nearly three acres of canvas—the greatest spread ever used by a circus. After a successful season (gross receipts: $400,000) Coup took the show out of wagons and put it on rails. Below: Barnum's advertising car (of a later date).

The 1873 show was the biggest yet and its daily running cost was $5,000, an unheard-of figure in those days.

At the season's end Barnum went to Europe to buy more wild animals and to pick up new acts for the show. Meanwhile Coup, a gambler with imagination, made a bold move. Without consulting Barnum he leased a property on 27th Street and Madison Avenue, New York, with the idea of transforming it into a gigantic indoor arena for their show.

P. T. Barnum's Great Roman Hippodrome (above) at Madison Square opened in April, 1874, before the largest crowd ever gathered in a New York building (about 10,000). The glittering performance began with the "Congress of Nations," a procession that, according to Barnum, "required nearly 1,000 persons, several hundred horses, besides elephants, llamas, camels, ostriches, etc." Following it came a series of races around the hippodrome track, and acrobatic and wire-walking feats.

Below is "The Grand Layout," an illustrator's conception of Barnum's Great Traveling World's Fair. The show gave three complete performances every day—morning, afternoon and evening—with an early morning parade thrown in. It boasted "Two Separate Rival Rings [a Coup innovation] under a vast center-pole pavillion with seats for 14,000." Other features were: "The Fiji Cannibals, Admiral Dot, An Endless Corps of Male and Female Riders," and "The Wonderful Talking Machine That Laughs, Sings and Talks in All Languages." Admission to the gaslit tents was fifty cents, children under nine half price, clergymen free.

Coup was largely responsible for the show's phenomenal success. He plastered the countryside with posters up to a distance of seventy-five miles from the showgrounds and persuaded the railroads to run excursion trains at cut rates from every town within range. But his greatest contribution was putting the show on rails in specially built cars of his own designing. (His system of loading and unloading was adopted by all railroad shows.) By rail the show could broaden the overnight jumps to distances of 100 miles or more and thus play only the larger and better paying towns. Furthermore it made it possible to haul a bigger and better show than ever.

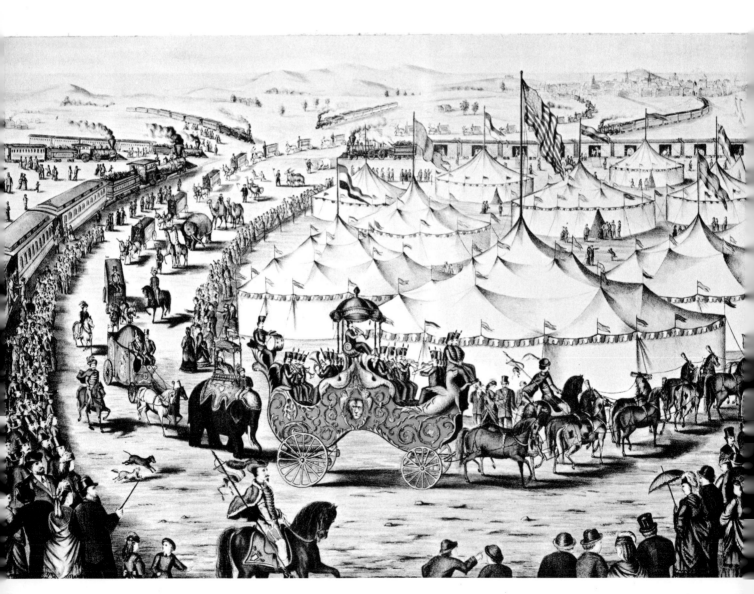

Above: A scene from "Barnum's Own Greatest Show On Earth," (from a program, 1878).

Below: "The Gigantic Orchestmelochor" (1879) "of such immense volume and power that its melodious strains can be heard for a distance of over five miles, giving the effect of a full orchestra."

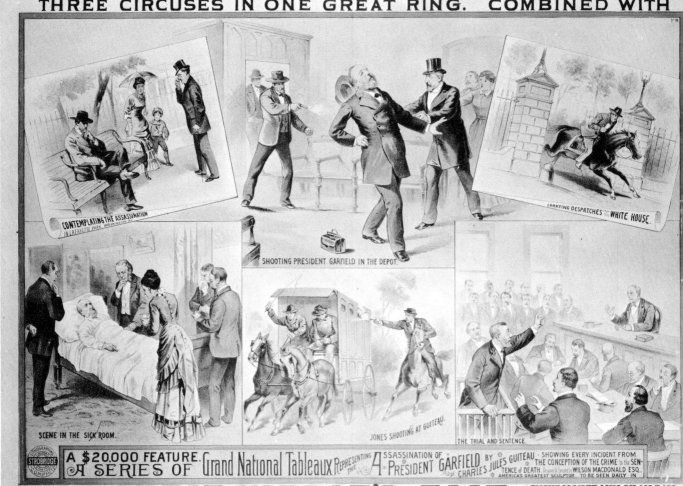

A Troupe of Genuine Male and Female Zulus.

Despite Coup's strong disapproval, Barnum split his enterprises in 1874 and leased his name and Traveling World's Fair to John V. (Pogey) O'Brien, a notorious grifter. In disgust Coup quit Barnum, took a two-year vacation and then returned to show business on his own. He founded and successfully operated the New York Aquarium, organized a tent show called the Equescurriculum ("A College of Trained Animals and Cephalodian Monsters of the Deep from the New York Aquarium"), and in 1879 began operation of his New United Monster Shows.

Featured during the 1882 season was a series of wax tableaux depicting the assassination of President Garfield and subsequent events (above). Also on the program were the Zulus (left), in answer to Barnum's group of Zulus.

Widely advertised by Coup's railroad show was his "Gigantic Devil Fish, 39½ feet including head, body and the longest tentacles . . . Preserved in Pure Alcohol." Coup offered to give $50,000 for one like it and $10,000 "for an equal to Mademoiselle Rinehart, the Only Female Lion Tamer, who enters a massive den of living wild lions and leopards and performs them like kittens."

Like other shows of that era Coup offered an assortment of attractions that would seem strange to a modern circus fan: A Japanese Art Gallery, a White Whale, the Imperial Barouche of Napoleon III, a Lightning Zouave Drill.

Coup's star began to set following a severe railroad wreck which forced him to close his show. Several comeback attempts failed, the last one as manager of a small animal show. Coup retired after that and died in semi-poverty in Florida in 1895.

J.A.BAILEY

Jim McGinnis, like many another small town boy of the last century, ran away and joined the circus when he was twelve but unlike most boys he did not return home after a few days. Jim stayed with it, assumed the name of his protector (Frederick H. Bailey) and as James Anthony Bailey became the greatest managerial genius and organizer the circus has ever known. A boy wonder, Bailey rose fast and at twenty-six was the proprietor of the Cooper and Bailey Circus, soon to be one of the largest railroad shows in the country.

In 1876 when Bailey was twenty-nine he took the show to San Francisco and then embarked on a chartered steamship for Australia. Never before had a circus of such size visited that continent. It was a two-ring affair with a large menagerie, side show and a full complement of skilled performers. The show twice toured Australia, played South Pacific, East Indian and South American ports, returning to New York after an absence of nearly three years.

Opposite page: An 1879 poster featuring the electric light (first used in Bailey's show).

Ten Times the Largest and Best Show on Earth!

St. Joseph, WEDNESDAY, | SURE One Day ONLY! | JULY 23

COOPER, BAILEY & CO.'S
GREAT
International Allied Shows !

Having just Returned from a Grand Three Years Triumphal Tour Around the World,
Traveling 67,000 Miles by Land and Sea, have CONSOLIDATED FOR
THIS SEASON ONLY, with the

GREAT LONDON CIRCUS
And SANGER'S ROYAL BRITISH MENAGERIE.
FORMING A FORMIDABLE COMBINATION.

TWO SHOWS!   A DOUBLE CIRCUS!   TWO MENAGERIES !

IN OPERATION DAY & NIGHT At Every Performance

Resplendent Redolent Refulgent

FAINTLY DESCRIBES THE WONDERFUL

ELECTRIC LIGHT !

The Public Mind Dazed !   The Great Invention !
ALL OF OUR VAST PAVILIONS
LIGHTED BY ELECTRICITY.
168,000 YARDS OF CANVAS
Are used in the manufacture of the CIRCUS, MENA-
GERIE AQUARIUM and MUSEUM TENTS, all of

Shortly after the show returned from Australia Bailey and his partner, James E. Cooper (left), bought Howes Great London Circus and Sanger's Royal British Menagerie. The merger created a tremendous circus and Barnum, who had had some rough sailing since Coup's departure, was keenly aware of the rival show. A bitter circus war between the two organizations came to a crisis when a baby elephant was born on March 10, 1880, at the Bailey winter quarters—the first one born in captivity in this country. Barnum promptly wired Bailey, offering him $100,000 for the greatly advertised attraction. Bailey's reply staggered the Bridgeport showman: A curt refusal followed by an avalanche of publicity quoting the telegram and captioned, "What Barnum Thinks of the Baby Elephant."

Barnum admitted that he had now met his master. The two men got together later that year and joined forces "in one mammoth combination."

Below: The Bridgeport winter quarters of the world-famous partnership.

At the top of the circus world stood Barnum, Bailey and Hutchinson in 1881. Cooper had sold his interest; Hutchinson was soon to drop out of the combine and the show became Barnum and Bailey.

 # Heyday of The Circus

The heyday of the American circus covered, roughly, a period of forty years which began in the 1880's with the formation of the great railroad shows and ended shortly after the first world war when the street parade began to fade out.

It was a time of glory in the sawdust and spangles world, of the two-mile-long magnificent parade with its multiple-horse teams, floats, calliopes, telescoping tableaux up to thirty feet in height and the ornate, beautifully carved band wagons, the most notable of which was the ten-ton, "Two Hemispheres," built at a cost of $40,000. But the parade is only part of the story.

It was a period that produced some of our finest performers, such as the equestrians James Robinson and Charles W. Fish of incomparable form; the spectacular leapers like Frank A. Gardiner, William H. Batcheller and John Worland who turned double somersaults over the backs of a row of elephants; the first great flyer, Ernest Clarke, who did a triple from the swinging bar to the hands of his brother and did it successfully for more than thirty years; the bicycle daredevils who looped the loop and jumped wide gaps in a runway at terrific speed, and the nationally known clowns, Billy Burke, Al Miaco, Spader Johnson and Frank (Slivers) Oakley.

The heyday saw the introduction of the first American three-ring circus (produced by Barnum and Bailey in 1881), but whether this was a step forward or not has been debated by circus lovers ever since. Many people believe that the three-ring, two-platform show is too large and bewildering—an opinion expressed in the cartoon on the right (from *Life*, 1889).

At any rate the competing circuses were soon forced to add another ring. This, of course, meant larger tents, greater equipment and more cars to haul them. By 1891 there were seven large railroad shows touring the country, the smallest of which were the Great Wallace and the Ringling Brothers shows with twenty cars each. Barnum and Bailey had 65 cars that year, Adam Forepaugh 52, Sells Brothers 42, John Robinson 35 and Walter L. Main 27.

Jack: HEAVENS! WHAT'S THE MATTER WITH YOUR EYES, BOB?
Bob: I'VE BEEN TO A THREE-RING CIRCUS.

In the heyday of the circus parade watchers got a full view of the "living serpents," for the wagons which carried them (always called "dens") were equipped with plate glass-enclosed sides. The larger shows boasted four or five of these dens. After the parade they were displayed in the menagerie.

An American contribution to the circus was the "steam organ," or calliope, which was invented in 1855 by J. C. Stoddard of Worcester, Massachusetts. A potentially lethal instrument because the boiler sometimes blew up from too much pressure, its traditional place in the parade was at the tail end.

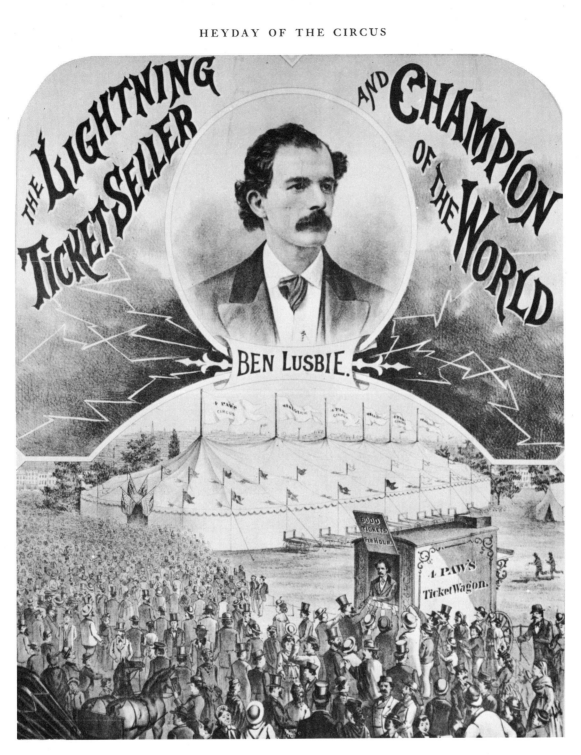

Ben Lusbie, "the quickest dispenser of show tickets in the world," was as much of an attraction as the star performers of the shows he worked and he received equal billing with them. A diminutive, slight, quick-tempered dynamo, Ben could sell more tickets than any two men could take. When he was with the Barnum show under the Coup regime he once sold 6,000 tickets in one hour. Later with Adam Forepaugh he got rid of 6,153 in an hour and three minutes. For this feat he was officially designated by the *National Police Gazette* as the champion ticket seller of the world.

One of the most graceful and thrilling acts of yesterday's circus was leaping, an acrobatic feat which was accomplished with the aid of an inclined running board, a springboard at the take-off and a landing pad at the finish. Between the springboard and the pad the leaper would turn one and sometimes two somersaults while soaring over a row of elephants or horses. Best of the leapers were Frank A. Gardiner, William H. Batcheller and John Worland, all of whom regularly did the double somersault over the lined-up animals.

A daily balloon ascension (opposite page) was featured by some circuses in the gaslit era. Barnum's "Professor" Donaldson took off from Chicago one day in 1875 and was never seen again.

MET PRINT N.Y.

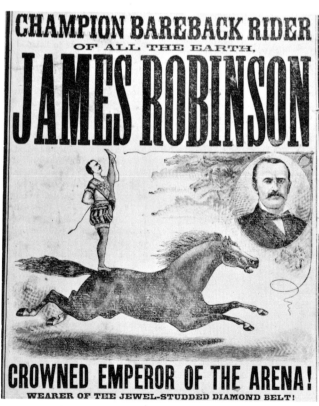

The greatest equestrian in the heyday of the circus was James Robinson, champion for forty-odd years and more than any other man responsible for founding the acrobatic school of bareback riding. Most of his competitors were still riding "pad" (i.e., with the aid of a pad covering the horse's back) when Robinson started his career in the 1850's. He never rode pad, always bareback, and it was largely because of his extraordinary feats on the uncovered back of his gray horse, Bull, that the pad riders faded from existence.

In 1856 when he was twenty-one and riding for Spalding and Rogers he turned twenty-three consecutive backward and forward somersaults over banners four feet wide without missing once. He always considered this to be his greatest feat.

The above picture shows him turning a backward somersault, his specialty. He would stand well back on the horse facing the tail and then turn it, catching the horse's back. He never missed.

84

Robinson was born James Michael Fitzgerald in Boston in 1835. He was adopted by John Robinson, circus owner, who gave the lad his name and taught him to ride. Young James was built for the riding ring. He never got above five feet, five but he was strong and nimble and had very small feet. Acrobatic riding was not unknown before his time but Robinson devised new tricks and brought the art to high degree. For years he was known as "The Man Who Rides." Charles W. Fish, another rider of great skill, was almost his equal but Robinson defeated him in a championship match. In 1889 he retired with his trophies (below) and lived until 1917.

WHAT A TRIFLE MAY EMBROIL NATIONS!

The enormous African elephant Jumbo had been the favorite of London's Zoological Gardens for eighteen years when Barnum in 1882 announced that he had bought the animal for $10,000 and was going to ship it to this country. The announcement touched off a furor of public indignation in England.

The international tiff inspired American cartoonist Thomas Nast to sketch the above scene in which the British Lion says to the American Eagle: "In the name of Queen Victoria, the Royal Family and over a million children, I demand his release." A reluctant Jumbo arrived here on April 9, 1882.

Jumbo's arrival was as spectacular as his career with the Barnum show was to be. After his removal from the steamship *Assyrian Monarch* he was hauled through the streets of New York (above) in a giant crate drawn by sixteen horses and pushed by two elephants. His measurements, as reported in *Leslie's Illustrated News*: 11 feet 6 inches high at the shoulders; 15 feet across the head from ear tip to ear tip; weight 6½ tons; trunk 7 feet. His daily fare consisted of 200 pounds of hay, two bushels of oats, one of biscuits, fifteen loaves of bread, three quarts of onions, five buckets of water, apples, oranges, figs, nuts, cakes, candies, and an occasional bottle of whiskey. (He could take down a quart in one gulp with no apparent effect.)

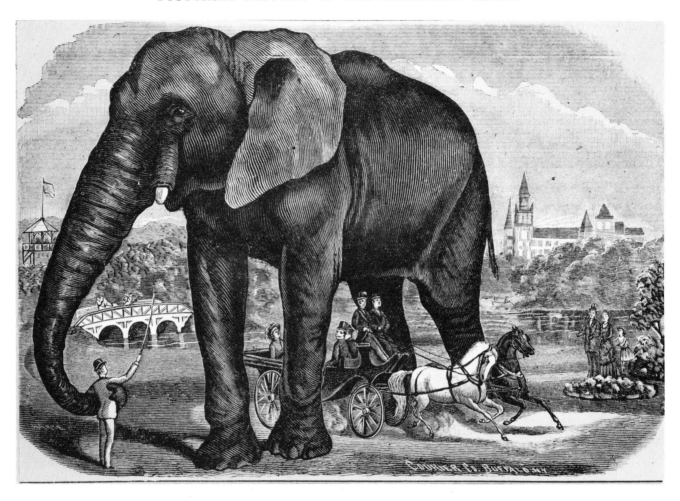

Nearly FIVE MILLION PEOPLE in this Country have already Seen, with growing Awe and Wonder,

ALL-FAMOUS AND GIGANTIC

"JUMBO"

And of all that vast number, not a single one disputes his tremendous eminence as

THE MIGHTY LORD OF ALL BEASTS
AND
ALONE THE SHOW OF SHOWS.

All concede him to be, beyond all question,

The Largest Living Quadruped on Earth

And since his arrival in America,

HE HAS GROWN SEVERAL INCHES IN HEIGHT, and INCREASED OVER A TON IN WEIGHT.

THIS TOWERING MONSTER
AMONG ALL THE HUGEST ELEPHANTS,
IS REALLY A HISTORIC MAMMOTH

The greatest single attraction of Barnum's circus career, Jumbo lived up to his advance billing, drew vast crowds and dominated the show for three and a half years. There were Jumbo cigars, Jumbo hats, fans, pies and stew. His name has since found a place in the English language as signifying anything of huge proportions.

Death came to the giant elephant on September 15, 1885, after the circus had finished its evening performance at St. Thomas, Ontario. Jumbo and a midget elephant, Tom Thumb, were walking along a railroad track when a freight train rounded a curve and ran into them. It hit Tom Thumb first and tossed him into a ditch. Then it struck Jumbo and stopped dead. He died a few minutes later of a fractured skull and internal injuries.

The pictures on the opposite page (from a circus pamphlet) depicting Jumbo's heroic efforts to save Tom Thumb, is Barnum's glamorized version of the accident and not the way it actually happened.

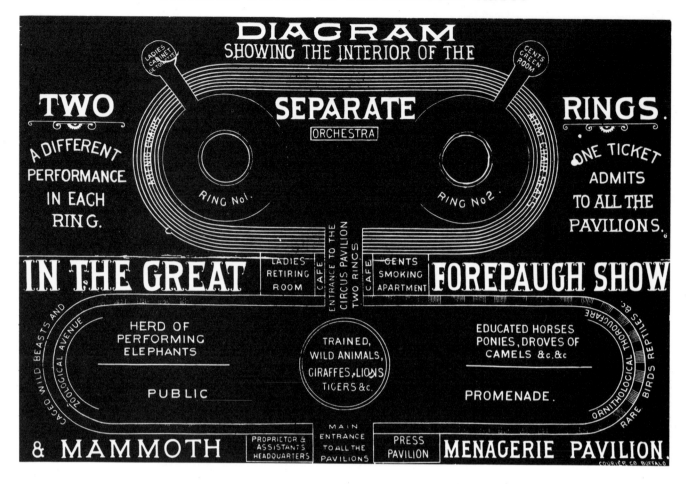

DIAGRAM SHOWING THE INTERIOR OF THE

TWO SEPARATE RINGS.

A DIFFERENT PERFORMANCE IN EACH RING.

ONE TICKET ADMITS TO ALL THE PAVILIONS.

RING No1.   ORCHESTRA   RING No2.

IN THE GREAT   FOREPAUGH SHOW

LADIES CABINET DE TOILETTE   GENTS GREEN ROOM

ARENA SEATS   ARM CHAIR SEATS

LADIES RETIRING ROOM   CAFE   ENTRANCE TO THE CIRCUS PAVILION TWO RINGS   CAFE   GENTS SMOKING APARTMENT

CAGED WILD BEASTS AND ZOOLOGICAL AVENUE

HERD OF PERFORMING ELEPHANTS

PUBLIC

TRAINED, WILD ANIMALS, GIRAFFES, LIONS TIGERS &c.

EDUCATED HORSES PONIES, DROVES OF CAMELS &c. &c

PROMENADE.

ORNITHOLOGICAL RARE BIRDS REPTILES &c THOROUGHFARE

& MAMMOTH   PROPRIETOR & ASSISTANTS HEADQUARTERS   MAIN ENTRANCE TO ALL THE PAVILIONS   PRESS PAVILION   MENAGERIE PAVILION.

COURIER CO BUFFALO

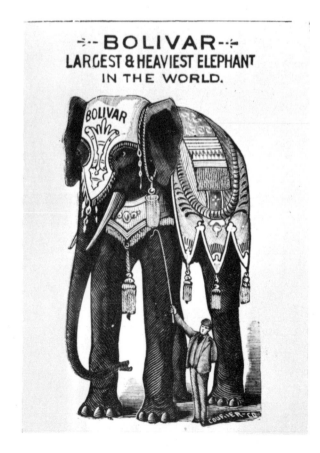

=·- BOLIVAR -·=
LARGEST & HEAVIEST ELEPHANT IN THE WORLD.

BOLIVAR

COURIER CO.

It made no difference to Barnum's rival, Adam Forepaugh, that Jumbo was truly the world's largest elephant. In 1883, at the height of Jumbo's fame, Forepaugh advertised that his elephant, Bolivar (left), was the biggest one in existence. His claim was never accepted by the public. Bolivar was a big tusker and became so dangerous that he was eventually given to the zoo in Philadelphia.

The Forepaugh show had only two rings in 1881 (above) when Barnum and Bailey launched their first three-ring circus, in Madison Square Garden. Not to be outdone, Forepaugh issued a "rat sheet" (a unique type of circus advertisement of savage attack and name calling) which accused Barnum of "Fraud! Falsehood! and Downright Deceit!" Barnum's New York parade did not have 100 cages, 20 elephants and hundreds of costumed people, as advertised, said Forepaugh. The correct number was 23 cages, 14 elephants and only 25 mounted paraders in uniform. "Note the Discrepancy," stated the rat sheet. "A Gross Exaggeration Without a Single Word of Truth."

Like most showmen of his time Adam Forepaugh had no hesitation about glorifying himself in couriers (publicity pamphlets) as the above picture points out. It shows Father Philadelphia welcoming native son Forepaugh back to the city after his supposed triumph over the Barnum show. "Well done, my son," said Father Philadelphia. (A notable exception to self-advertising was James A. Bailey, a shy, retiring man who loathed the spotlight but was a master at publicizing his circus.)

An unusual act in the '80's was Sells Brothers' "$18,000 Herd of Six Performing Colorado Cattle, the Only Ones Ever Educated and Exhibited in the Ring. Others Have Tried to Imitate Them But Have Utterly and Ridiculously Failed."

There were few people in the United States in 1881 who did not know about Louise Montague (left), the announced winner of Forepaugh's $10,000 contest for the most beautiful woman who was willing to put herself on exhibition by leading his street pageant, Lalla Rookh's Departure from Delhi (above).

For two seasons Miss Montague, a bosomy variety actress who had been chosen in a fixed contest and never saw the $10,000 (she got $100 a week), led the pageant and drew great crowds. For once, Forepaugh out-Barnumed Barnum in getting national publicity. The streets were packed wherever the siren showed. In Chicago a crowd shattered the windows of the Western Union office and a man fell out of a second floor window and broke his neck. Receipts made new records. Forepaugh netted $240,000 in 1881, $260,000 the next season.

A GENUINE SOUTHERN SLAVE SINGING BAND OF CAMP-MEETING MELODISTS

Above: Forepaugh's "Troupe of Genuine Old-Time Plantation Darkies," a feature in 1883.

Below: Forepaugh's eight-acre winter quarters facing Lehigh Avenue in Philadelphia.

Mass production of the highly colored poster, made possible by the invention of the lithographic steam press, gave the circus a natural advertising medium in the 1870's. Circuses ordered posters by the thousands, tried to outdo each other in papering the countryside. Not all of these posters were used for advance billing, however. Many were in the form of rat sheets, such as the one below.

In this poster Barnum (as the Ox) makes use of Aesop's Fable to sneer at his arch rival Adam Forepaugh (as the Frog) who, in trying to blow himself up to Barnum's size, is about to "go bust."

Forepaugh responded with a rat sheet of his own in which he depicted himself as a giant towering above his tiny rivals, Barnum, Bailey and Hutchinson. It was captioned "A Giant Among the Pigmys."

THE FROG AND THE OX.

An Ox, grazing in a swampy meadow, chanced to set his foot among a parcel of young Frogs and crushed nearly the whole brood to death. One that escaped, ran off to his mother with the dreadful news; "And, O mother!" said he, "it was a beast, such a big four-footed beast, that did it." "Big?" quoth the old Frog, "how big? was it big" and she puffed herself out to a great degree "as big as this?" "Oh!" said the little one, "a great deal bigger than that." "Well, was it so big?" and she swelled out more. "Indeed, mother, but it was; and if you were to burst yourself you could never reach half its size." Provoked at such a disparagement of her powers, the old Frog made one more trial, and burst herself indeed.
So Men are ruined by attempting a greatness to which they have no claim.---*Aesop's Fables.*

THIS OLD *FOUR-CLAWED* FROG ALWAYS WAS TOO FULL OF WIND AND "BUSTED" IN THE VAIN ATTEMPT TO PUFF HIMSELF UP TO THE PROPORTIONS OF THE GIGANTIC **BARNUM OX.**

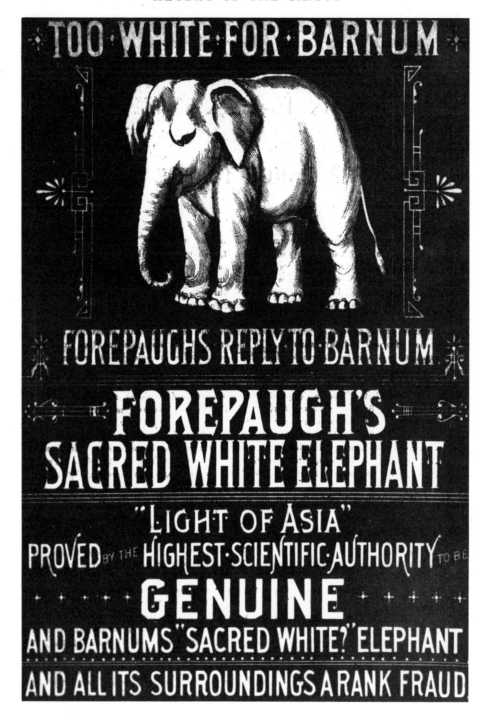

Barnum's acquisition of the "Sacred White Elephant," Toung Taloung, gave Forepaugh another opportunity to continue the rat sheet war. The animal had been bought in Burma by Barnum's agents for $75,000 the year before Jumbo's death. Before its arrival here in 1884 it was widely heralded as an extremely rare specimen—pure, milky white in color. Toung Taloung turned out to be a flop.

He was not white at all and looked very much like any other elephant except for a few pinkish spots around his ears. Barnum was greatly disappointed but not Forepaugh who responded by having one of his elephants secretly whitewashed and billing it as a genuine sacred white elephant. In addition he had the above rat sheet printed, charging that Barnum's elephant was a rank fraud.

ALL QUARTERS OF THE GLOBE CONTRIBUTE TO OUR MENAGERIE.
ARRIVAL AT NEW YORK & UNLOADING ANIMALS FROM THE STEAMSHIP
INDIA CHINA & JAPAN WAREHOUSE
ORIENTAL STEAMSHIP NEW YORK
OCEANICA

John Robinson

Among the shows competing against Barnum and Forepaugh when the two giants were battling each other across the country was the John Robinson Circus (shown above, unloading animals from a chartered steamship).

It was founded by John Robinson (left) who took over a small wagon show about 1840, developed it into a big money-maker and passed on the management to his son, John G., in 1870. The show was supreme in the South before and after the Civil War despite its Yankee ownership. (Old John was born in upstate New York; winter quarters were in Cincinnati.) It stayed in the family, continued to flourish under the management of grandson, John G., and in the 1890's boasted "three generations of circus kings" and called itself the "Greatest of All American Shows." Ringling Brothers leased the show in 1898 but the Robinsons resumed control the following year. It went off the road in 1912, was revived four years later and ended its long career (under Ringling management again) in 1930.

THE GREAT INTER-OCEAN
LARGEST & BEST SHOW ON EARTH.

Like every other large show of its time the Great Inter-Ocean claimed to be the largest and best on earth with the best acts, biggest menagerie and rarest animals, such as the Egyptian Bovalapus (below), a name that must have been picked out of a press agent's hat. The Great Inter-Ocean, however, was a big winner during its brief career.

Organized by showman John B. Doris in 1883, it ran until 1888 when heavyweight champion John L. Sullivan became a partner. The fighter, then at the height of his pugilistic and drinking fame, was supposed to appear in a sparring bout at each performance. But he went on so many drinking sprees that Doris, in disgust, closed in mid-season.

THE GREAT EGYPTIAN BOVALAPUS.

SIDE SHOW

"There is a superabundance of ugliness and deformity which one is obliged to see without running after and nosing it out," wrote Horace Greeley in 1852 following a visit to Barnum's Museum where he had gazed upon a pair of flat-headed Mexican Indians billed as the Aztec Children. In so writing Greeley expressed a minority opinion. For the public display of human abnormality in its various forms, however grotesque, has always fascinated rather than repelled the majority of people.

The average man, inherently curious, is naturally attracted by human oddities. Moreover, the sight of a dwarf, a giant or a true monstrosity such as a double-bodied man, gives him, perhaps, a feeling of superiority over his more unfortunate brethren, makes him more contented with his own lot.

Ever since the first freak was exhibited in this country (a maiden dwarf, Emma Leach, who was shown in Boston in 1771 for one shilling a look) people have paid to look upon human oddities.

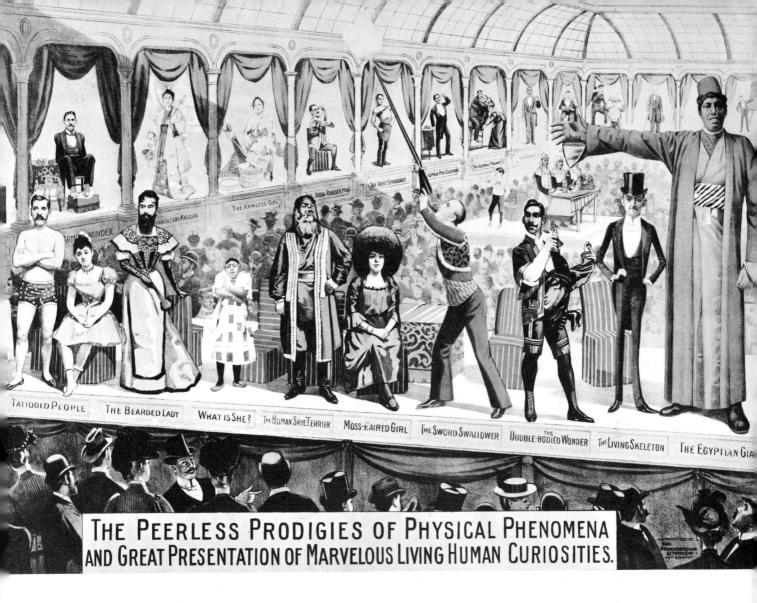

TATTOOED PEOPLE · THE BEARDED LADY · WHAT IS SHE? · THE HUMAN SKYE TERRIER · MOSS-HAIRED GIRL · THE SWORD SWALLOWER · THE DOUBLE-BODIED WONDER · THE LIVING SKELETON · THE EGYPTIAN GIA

THE PEERLESS PRODIGIES OF PHYSICAL PHENOMENA AND GREAT PRESENTATION OF MARVELOUS LIVING HUMAN CURIOSITIES.

Freaks, like animals, were at first exhibited singly in taverns and inns, later in museums along with an assortment of inanimate curiosities. These early museums were more like side shows than institutions for art and antiques, and freaks were shown in them (in limited numbers) long before Barnum's day. But it was Barnum, as we have seen, who first realized the drawing power of freaks and brought them into prominence in his American Museum and later in his tented shows.

The side show, now fading from the circus scene, was once an elaborate show-within-a-show and an important part of every large circus, as the above Barnum and Bailey 1898 poster demonstrates. The big circus was then playing in England and offered some thirty human oddities in its side show.

Right: Etta Lake, a rubber-faced girl of 1900 vintage.

99

LITH.BY CURRER & IVES, Entered according to act of Congress in the year 1860, by Currier & Ives, in the Clerk's Office of the District Court for the Southern Dist of N.Y. 152 NASSAU ST NEW YORK.

"CHANG" AND "ENG"
THE WORLD RENOWNED UNITED
SIAMESE TWINS.

NOW EXHIBITING AT BARNUM'S AMERICAN MUSEUM, NEW YORK.

Remarkable among freaks were the original Siamese Twins, Chang and Eng, who were joined at the breastbone when they were born in Siam in 1811 and remained so until their death at Mt. Airy, North Carolina, in 1874. No less remarkable was their career. Ten years after their arrival in this country (in 1829) they settled down in Wilkes County, North Carolina, became American citizens and in 1843 married Sarah and Adelaide Yates, daughters of a local farmer, in a double wedding (above). They reared some twenty-two children, operated separated farms and homes a mile apart (they spent three days with one wife, three days with the other) and earned the respect of the community as hard-working farmers. Occasionally the twins went on the road again and for a short time were exhibited at Barnum's Museum (opposite page).

Although they were identical twins they differed in physique and character. Chang was an inch shorter than his brother and was more aggressive. He liked to take a nip now and then. Eng was a teetotaler but did not feel the effects of Chang's drinking. Sometimes they quarrelled and went for long periods without speaking to each other.

The twins died one night in January, 1874. Chang was the first to go. Before a doctor could be summoned Eng followed him.

The Wild Men of Borneo were captured after a deadly struggle by a ship's crew in search of water. They were of a distinct human race, spoke no intelligible tongue and uttered a strange mixture of gibberish and guttural howls. So wild and ferocious were they that they could easily subdue tigers.

So stated a Barnum courier in 1882. Barnum's Wild Men were born Hiram W. and Barney Davis and were billed as Plutano and Waino. (Photo at left shows the brothers standing between their guardian, Hanaford A. Warner of Waltham, Massachusetts.)

They were good natured, gentle little fellows of subnormal mentality. They were really strong, however, and on display would amuse the crowds by picking up six-foot men with ease. Hiram was born in Long Island, Barney in England. A tombstone in Mount Vernon, Ohio, marks their grave with this inscription:

LITTLE MEN

Hiram W. Davis	1825-1905
Barney Davis	1827-1912

THE AZTEC CHILDREN.

The hawk-faced, speechless Aztec Children (Maximo and Bartola) were featured in Barnum's Museum in the 1850's. Supposedly brother and sister, they were married while on tour in England in 1867.

The Infant Esau, son of the Bearded Lady, inherited his mother's hirsute gifts.

The four-year-old lad is shown above, already sprouting a beard and a thick thatch on his back.

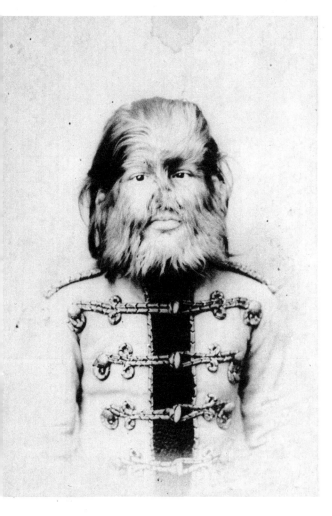

On this page are shown some outstanding examples of abnormal hair growth—a prize sought by all side show managers. Above is Jo Jo, the Dog-Faced Boy (born Theodore Peteroff in Russia) who was first exhibited here in 1885. Sometimes billed as the Human Sky Terrier, he had long silky hair on his cheeks and forehead. When his body was wrapped in a blanket with only his head visible, his resemblance to a sky terrier was startling.

Above, right: Moung Phoset and his mother, Mah Phoon (in 1887), both of whom were enveloped from head to foot in a wavy mass of hair. Even their noses were hair covered.

Right: Krao, the Siamese Missing Link, as a young girl. She was totally covered by hair, had cheek pouches and lacked cartilege in the nose. Krao was of normal mentality and was a popular attraction in adult life for many years in this country.

Charles B. Tripp (above) and his legless friend Eli Bowen (above, right) made a strange sight when they rode a tandem bicycle, which they often did for recreation after hours. Bowen in front would do the steering, Tripp would supply the leg power.

"Watch your step," Trip would say and the invariable reply would be "Keep your hands off me." Such was the banter between the armless and legless pals who were exhibited side by side for many years in various shows.

Tripp was remarkably adroit with his feet and toes. He could feed and shave himself, write letters, light and smoke cigarettes, and was a passable portrait painter. He was intelligent and well educated.

The good natured Bowen stood two feet, eight inches on his legless feet and weighed 140 pounds. In 1870 he married a pretty girl of sixteen named Mattie Haight who bore him three children.

Below: Tripp and Bowen take a spin on the tandem.

A rare freak was Francesco A. Lentini who had an extra leg growing out of his hip. Born in Sicily in 1889, Francesco used his third limb for walking and running up to the age of six. After that his body started to outgrow the unwanted leg and eventually it became six inches shorter than the other two. He could move it, however, and one of his stunts was to kick a football with it. Due to the extra leg he ate about fifteen per cent more food than the average man and weighed 165 pounds. Two-legged, he would have weighed about 150. Lentini married a normal woman and was the father of two boys and a girl. He was with many shows, among them Ringling-Barnum, Walter L. Main and Buffalo Bill.

Myrtle Corbin (right) was one leg up on Lentini. She had four altogether, two of normal size and two smaller ones between them. According to a pamphlet written in 1882 when she was first exhibited, she had two sets of organs below the waist.

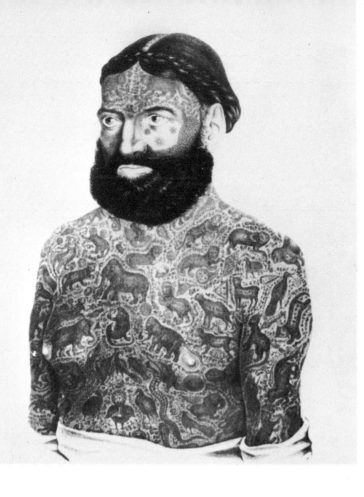

Captain Georg Constantine, a Greek Albanian who was exhibited by Barnum in the 1870's, was probably the most completely tattooed person who ever lived. Scarcely a quarter of an inch from his scalp to the soles of his feet was free from designs. They were on his eyelids, genitals, the interior of his ears, beneath the hair on his head and between his fingers and toes. The 388 symmetrically arranged designs made him look as if he were covered by a transparent blue shawl.

According to the Captain, he received the ornaments by force when he was taken prisoner by "the Chinese Tartars" in Burma, the ordeal lasting three months (note cut, below). Tattoo experts agreed that the designs were of Burmese style but thought it more likely that the Captain had paid a native master to be tattooed for purposes of exhibition.

Opposite page: An oddity among human oddities was Miss Fanny Mills, an attractive blonde who wore size 30 shoes (from an 1885 periodical).

NINTH AND ARCH MUSEUM

THAT GIRL FROM OHIO!

MISS FANNIE MILLS, WHO HAS

THE BIGGEST FEET ON EARTH.

No. 30 SHOE THE SMALLEST SHE CAN WEAR.
HER FEET ARE HER FORTUNE.

No person ever had so much understanding. Her foot only excelled by the foot of a mountain. Each shoe large enough to go to sea in. The late lamented Jumbo would have been proud of his little foot had he seen Miss Mills.

A BOON FOR POOR BACHELORS!

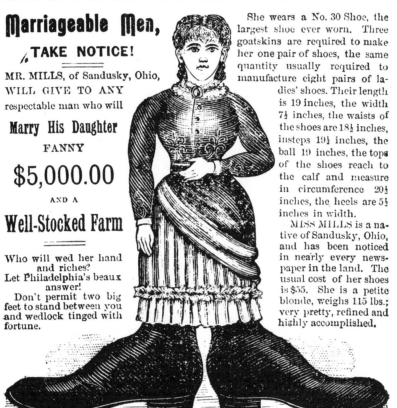

Marriageable Men,

TAKE NOTICE!

MR. MILLS, of Sandusky, Ohio, WILL GIVE TO ANY respectable man who will

Marry His Daughter

FANNY

$5,000.00

AND A

Well-Stocked Farm

Who will wed her hand and riches? Let Philadelphia's beaux answer! Don't permit two big feet to stand between you and wedlock tinged with fortune.

She wears a No. 30 Shoe, the largest shoe ever worn. Three goatskins are required to make her one pair of shoes, the same quantity usually required to manufacture eight pairs of ladies' shoes. Their length is 19 inches, the width 7½ inches, the waists of the shoes are 18½ inches, insteps 19½ inches, the ball 19 inches, the tops of the shoes reach to the calf and measure in circumference 20½ inches, the heels are 5½ inches in width.

MISS MILLS is a native of Sandusky, Ohio, and has been noticed in nearly every newspaper in the land. The usual cost of her shoes is $55. She is a petite blonde, weighs 115 lbs.; very pretty, refined and highly accomplished.

"The Old Woman Who Lived in a Shoe"

Would have rented out apartments if she had resided in one of MISS MILLS'. Her feet are too big to ride in a passenger coach and she has to travel in a box-car.

CHICAGO GIRLS MUST YIELD THE PALM, WHERE ARE THE ST. LOUIS BEAUTIES? WHAT WILL THE BOSTON LADIES SAY?

BY COMPARISON PHILADELPHIA DAMSELS ARE CINDERELLAS. A PAIR OF HER SHOES COST AN ORDINARY MAN'S MONTH'S SALARY.

WHO WILL WED THIS BUCKEYE BEAUTY, $5000 AND THE WELL STOCKED FARM? A GENUINE BONA FIDE OFFER.

The Science-puzzling Phenomenon, the ELASTIC SKIN MAN.
CROSSMAN AND WIFE, the Yankee Whittlers. ANNIE NELSON, the Fairy Queen.
PROF. GEIS, the Caricaturist, in Shakspere's Seven Ages.
PEARL EVARTS, Albino Beauty, with her Talking Bird. MONS. EVARTS, the Wizard of the West.
SARCO, LEMO and DRESO, Genuine Hindoo War Chieftains, "from the Land of the Jungle."

THANKSGIVING SPECIALTY CO.

TWENTY STRONG.

SPECIAL THANKSGIVING DAY PERFORMANCES,

Beginning at 9.30 A. M. and given continuously every hour until 10.30 P. M.
ADMISSION AND A SEAT, ONE DIME. PERFORMANCES HOURLY.
Doors open 1 P. M. and 6.30 daily; Saturday, 10.30 A. M.

If ever a man deserved the name of bonehead it was Billy Wells (above) whose skull was of triple thickness—two inches in the center with the sutures completely ossified, according to a doctor who examined him. A side show performer with many circuses, Billy would stand without blinking while blocks of granite placed on his head were broken by the blows of a sledge hammer. Between his head and the stone there was only a thin cloth cushion to prevent his scalp from being cut. Another stunt of Billy's was to let his assistant break an inch-and-a-half-thick pine plank across his head. Years of absorbing such blows seemed to have no effect on him. He died at the age of seventy in 1910.

Another of abnormal skull was the Long-Head Man (above, right), who was shown in the 1880's.

No side show of the last century was complete without its Ossified Man (right). A celebrated one was Jonathan R. Bass who is said to have turned to stone before he died.

Unique among the strange people was Count Orloff, a physiological marvel beyond compare, for he was not only ossified but he was transparent as well. He was so translucent that the circulation of his blood could be seen and studied. When a light was placed against his breast a newspaper held across his back could be easily read.

Born Ivannow Wladislaus Von Dziarski-Orloff in Budapest in 1864, he began to fail in strength at fourteen. At eighteen his limbs could no longer support his body and he took to a chair. He never left it. The curved condition of his limbs was caused by softening of the bones and the muscles drawing them into that shape. The Count was never without pain and would smoke an opium pipe to relieve his suffering (note above photo). He was exhibited at the Royal College of Medicine in Berlin for three years and was first shown in this country in 1893. He died in 1904.

The photo on the right, dated 1882, is identified only as "The Living Half Man, aged 18." Freaks of this nature are not too uncommon and rank in the middle salary bracket—from $50 to $100 a week.

HISTORY AND MEDICAL DESCRIPTION
OF THE
TWO-HEADED GIRL.

ROY LANCE & PURDELL

Joined twins have always rated high in the salary scale, earning in some cases up to $1,000 a week. Millie and Christine, a Negro pair who danced, sang duets (one was a soprano, the other a contralto) and accompanied themselves on guitars, averaged $600 a week in the 1880's.

The girls were born slaves in North Carolina in 1851 and were exhibited by Barnum under the misleading title of the Two-Headed Girl. (The above pictures show Barnum's version, and a photograph of the pair taken in 1880.)

The twins were joined at the back, more closely than the Siamese Twins, and their intestines were united. They possessed a common sensory nerve system in the legs, both feeling a touch on any of the four limbs. Christine (the one on the right) was the stronger and by bending could lift up her sister.

The twins were shown throughout the United States and twice toured Europe. On one trip abroad they were received by Queen Victoria (left).

"The most remarkable human twins that have ever approached maturity," said the *Scientific American* of the sixteen-year-old Toccis Twins when they arrived in this country in 1891. They were advertised as "The Greatest Human Phenomenon Ever Seen Alive," and they probably were, for unlike all other joined twins the Toccis had but one pair of legs and were as close to being a two-headed person as anything nature has ever produced.

Born of normal parents (right) in Turin, Italy, they had nine normal brothers and sisters.

Above the waist they were two persons, below it one (two chest bones and four nipples but only one abdomen). One mouth could eat enough to satisfy the entire organism; one could sleep while the other was awake. They had difficulty in walking because each leg was governed by its own brain. They could write and draw skillfully, one using his right hand, the other his left. On tour in the United States the Toccis were paid $1,000 a week.

LITH. BY CURRIER & IVES.

162 NASSAU ST NEW YORK

WHAT IS IT?—OR "MAN MONKEY".
ON EXHIBITION AT BARNUM'S MUSEUM, NEW YORK.

Barnum's "What Is It?" was a weird-looking Negro with a cone-shaped, tufted head who was born William H. Jackson in New Jersey in 1842. Zip, as he was known, was first shown in 1859 and trouped continuously for sixty-seven years—perhaps longer than any freak in circus history. Zip was a good-natured imbecile who enjoyed being exhibited. Grinning continuously, he believed he owned the circus and had hired everybody in it.

Opposite page: One of the fattest of the fat ladies was Miss Jane Campbell, the "Connecticut Giantess" who weighed 628 pounds at eighteen.

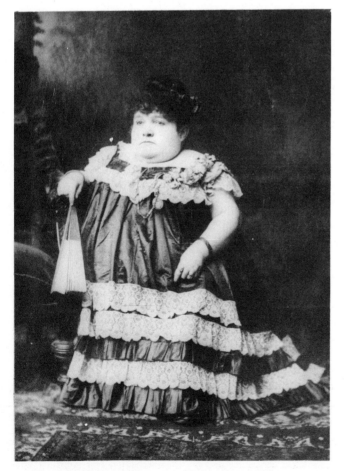

John Hanson Craig of Kentucky (above) may have been the heaviest man in history. Statistics on his porcine progress reveal that he weighed 77 pounds at eleven months, 206 at two years, 405 at thirteen and 601 at twenty-one. He then stood six feet, five inches but continued to grow in girth: 725 pounds at twenty-five, 806 at thirty, 907 (his maximum weight) at thirty-seven. Craig died a year later (in 1894), leaving a child and a 122-pound widow.

Virginia-born Carrie Akers (left) had the double peculiarity of being a fat lady *and* a dwarf. She was only thirty-five inches high but weighed close to 300 pounds.

On the opposite side of the weight scale was James W. Coffey, the Skeleton Dude (above, left). Coffey was of average height but was never able to get above seventy pounds.

Shown above is Barnum and Bailey's Big-Toed, Big-Fingered Boy, as he looked in 1892.

The so-called Elephant Boys (below) were features in many of the old-time side shows.

The smallest adult midget ever exhibited was, in all probability, Lucia Zarate (above) who, when fully grown was twenty inches high—give or take an inch—and weighed about five pounds. Her tiny waist measured fourteen inches, her forearm two and a half inches and her arm was eight inches long. Lucia was born in San Carlos, Mexico, in 1864, came to this country at the age of twelve and was on tour almost continually until 1890 when she died as a result of exposure while on a stalled train in a blizzard near Truckee, California. She was vivacious, intelligent and perfectly formed in every particular.

Almost equalling Lucia in minuteness (but not in mentality) was Princess Weenie Wee, a tiny colored girl. The photo on the left, taken in 1908, shows the Princess and her sister stepping off a trolley car in New York. Editor Arthur Brisbane interviewed the Princess and later wrote that she was so small a good-sized rat could carry her off.

Anna Swan (shown above with Barnum's group of giants and midgets) was a comely seven-footer who married Martin Bates, the Kentucky Giant, and retired with him to their Ohio farm in 1874.

They built a house to size. The rooms were fourteen feet from floor to ceiling, the doors nine feet high, and all furniture was made to order. A pair of Clysdale horses drew their huge carriage.

One of the tallest giants of recent years was George Augur, shown here with his wife and two midgets. He stood just short of eight feet in his stocking feet but with high-heeled boots and high hat gave the appearance of being nine feet tall. (Few, if any giants, ever topped eight feet despite side show claims. Minus boots and hat they rarely went over seven and a half feet.) If Augur was not *the* tallest he was certainly the most talented giant. He was a competent actor and author of the sketch,

"Jack the Giant Killer," in which he starred in vaudeville. Augur was born in Cardiff, Wales, in 1883 and quite naturally became known as "The Cardiff Giant" when he signed with Barnum and Bailey in England. When the show returned to America in 1903 Augur came with it and remained here. For several seasons he was the side show's main attraction, featured as "Positively the Tallest Man On Earth." The 360-pound giant died of acute indigestion on November 30, 1922, in New York City.

Mlle Zenobia.

Featured in the old-time side shows were the so-called "Circassians" who were supposed to represent the purest white stock of the Caucasian race. Many of these freaks were albinos who let their hair grow long and soaked it in stale beer to make it stand up. Above: Mlle. Zenobia (a blonde), the Albino Twins and "Unize," the Circassian Wonder.

The Seven Southerland Sisters, daughters of a Lockport, New York, farmer, were long-haired wonders who appeared in vaudeville and side shows during the 1880's. They played musical instruments and sang, and made a small fortune by lending their names to a hair tonic company. The last of the sisters, Grace, died on January 19, 1946.

Above: The pony, Chief, whose tail was over ten feet long.

Below: Thomas Wilkinson and his five-foot beard graced the side show platform for many years.

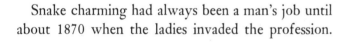

Snake charming had always been a man's job until about 1870 when the ladies invaded the profession.

In the heyday of the circus no side show was complete without its strong man and fire eater.

Below: An advertising card (Forepaugh Sells) featuring both menagerie and side show attractions.

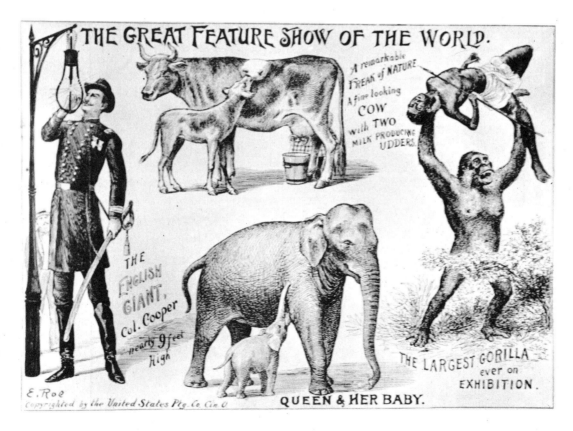

In extremely rare cases nature produces a terrible malformation in the form of a double-bodied person. Nature's intent to create twins misfires and the result (as once described) is "not one child and not two children, but more than one, yet not two."

Such were Jean and Jacques Libbera (above two photos) and the Hindu, Piramel and Sami (left).

Of more recent date was Libbera who was born in Rome in 1884 and shown by Barnum and Bailey in 1907. His parasitic body, Jacques, was almost perfect as far as it went. It had arms, legs, hands and feet with nails growing upon the toes and fingers. An X-ray examination revealed a strong bone structure and a rudimentary head imbedded in the normal body. The touching of one body was immediately felt by the other and the circulation of blood from the normal body furnished nourishment for both.

Libbera was married and the father of four normal children. Scientists who examined him pronounced him the greatest anomaly of nature ever known.

More typical of the side show are the freaks shown on this page: A rubber-faced man, a pair of achrondroplastic (imperfectly proportioned) dwarfs and (below) a girl with stump arms and legs.

The sensational preachers Thomas De Witt Talmage (above) and Henry Ward Beecher (opposite page) were ridiculed in this side show cartoon, "The Rival Shows in Brooklyn" (from *Puck*, 1878).

Talmage once visited Bowery sin dens in disguise and preached about his experiences from the pulpit.

Beecher, equally sensational and considered a hypocrite by many, was brought to trial for adultery.

-1932-

RINGLING BROTHERS AND BARI

RILEY COMBINED CIRCUS SIDE SHOW.

If William F. Cody had never gone into show business and established the Wild West Show he would still have a prominent niche in the history of the West as Buffalo Bill—Indian fighter, frontiersman, Chief of Army Scouts and professional buffalo hunter. The handsome, long-haired westerner became a nationally famous character before he was thirty because of his exploits on the plains (with an assist by Ned Buntline, a dime-novel writer who made him the hero of his tales). He came East in the seventies, enchanted everyone who met him and was thoroughly lionized in Chicago and New York. At this time he made his first stage appearance.

Buffalo Bill starred in a series of western melodramas but the stage bored him. What he wanted to show the country was something bigger than a mere stage show, an action-packed spectacle with horses, Indians and cowboys that would portray the real Wild West. He discussed the idea at length with Buntline, press agent John M. Burke and Nate Salsbury, an experienced showman. The result was the opening on May 17, 1883 at the Fair Grounds in Omaha of "The Wild West, Rocky Mountain and Prairie Exhibition," a show of circus proportions co-featuring Buffalo Bill and the trick shot artist, Dr. W. F. Carver. It was the first Wild West show.

The success of Buffalo Bill's show gave rise to numerous other Wild West outfits. One of the largest was Pawnee Bill's Wild West, formed in 1887. Pawnee Bill (Gordon W. Lillie) was a buffalo hunter, Indian agent and interpreter for the Pawnee tribe in Oklahoma. He first became interested in show business when he furnished a group of Pawnee braves for Buffalo Bill's stage and Wild West shows.

The Wild West shows stressed continuous action —trick riding and roping, races, battles between Indians and cowboys and most of all, exhibitions of sharpshooting. At this there was none better than Annie Oakley, famed as "Little Sure Shot" (left).

Annie was born on a farm in Darke County, Ohio, in 1860 and would probably have remained there in obscurity had it not been for her remarkable gift with rifle, shotgun and six-gun. At twelve she was a market hunter and could shoot the head off a running quail. In her teens she defeated Frank Butler, a great exhibition marksman. Butler fell in love with her and they were married. Soon established as the best marksmanship team in the country, they joined the Buffalo Bill show in 1885. For the next seventeen years Annie's act was the first in the show, following right after the Grand Review. (Butler gave up shooting, became her manager.)

Annie shot glass balls from the back of a running horse (below), shot holes in the pips of playing cards, knocked ashes off cigarettes held in the mouth. Little Sure Shot never missed.

These cartoons originally appeared in *Puck* in the spring of 1887 when Buffalo Bill's Wild West invaded England, then celebrating Queen Victoria's Golden Jubilee. How, wondered *Puck*, would British society receive the Indians and rough-hewn plainsmen, and (right) would Buffalo Bill and Chief Red Shirt look like this when they returned to America?

The tour, under the management of Buffalo Bill's astute partner, Nate Salsbury, turned out to be a huge success. England had never before seen a Wild West show and the stands were packed at almost every performance.

This was the first of three trips the show was to make to England and the continent. The final one began in 1902 and lasted four years. On this tour the German Crown Prince (later Kaiser Wilhelm II) allowed Annie Oakley to shoot a cigarette out of his mouth. Years later during World War I, Annie said, "I wish I'd missed that day."

133

A better than fair shot was Buffalo Bill, shown above at his famous stunt of shooting glass balls tossed aloft by his adopted son, Johnny Baker.

The scene below was described in the program as "The Attack on a Settler's Cabin and Rescue by Buffalo Bill and a Band of Cowboys."

It is unlikely that any vehicle in history ever survived as many attacks as the old Concord coach from Deadwood during its more than thirty-year existence with the Buffalo Bill show.

Right: A program illustration of the coach in action. The twice daily set-to was described as "Attack on the Deadwood Mail Coach by Indians, Repulsed by the Indians, and rescue of the stage, passengers and mail by Buffalo Bill and his attendant cowboys, scouts and frontiersmen."

Below is a photograph of the famous coach. On the horse sits the Indian, Iron Tail. Buffalo Bill, then toward the end of his career, stands beside the coach. The driver is Colorado Jack. Facing the rear is Bert Schenck, cowboy.

The Famous Original WILD WEST AND GREAT 4 PAW SHOW

Adam Forepaugh, like many circus owners of the Buffalo Bill era, took advantage of the current western vogue and added a Wild West unit to his circus, as the above 1887 handbill indicates. (The accompanying woodcut shows a group of Indians being run down by cowboys on the hippodrome track.) Forepaugh featured Captain Adam H. Bogardus (left), the Champion Wing Shot of America. The Captain earned the title in an official contest held in 1871 and successfully defended it for years.

The early Wild West shows were unlike the circus in that they had no side shows, freaks or clowns and they played at fairgrounds without a top. In time, however, the shows became less woolly and took on much of the character of the circus.

Mr VAN AMBURGH
in the Grand Spectacle of CHARLEMAGNE nightly represented
at the THEATRE ROYAL DRURY LANE.

D̲R̲ W. F. CARVER.
CHAMPION RIFLE SHOT OF THE WORLD.

When the Ringling brothers of Baraboo, Wisconsin, opened their first show under canvas in their home town on May 19, 1884, the event caused no stir at all in the circus world. There is no reason why it should have, no reason why anyone could possibly foresee that before twenty years had passed the pitifully small wagon show would equal in size its sole competitor, Barnum and Bailey's Greatest Show on Earth, and would eventually absorb it.

For the Ringling show in 1884, despite its grandiloquent title, "The Yankee Robinson & Ringling Bros. Great Double Shows, Circus and Caravan," was just another one of the many one-ring circuses that were sprouting throughout the land. Why did this show, organized by country boys without circus tradition and so small that its entire equipment and personnel could be moved in ten ordinary farm wagons, become the greatest the world has ever seen?

The humorist, George Ade, gave one good reason when he said, "They found the business in the hands of vagabonds and put it in the hands of gentlemen. They . . . became the circus kings of the world by adopting and observing the simple rule that it is better to be straight than to be crooked."

The parents of the future showmen were August Rüngeling and Salome Juliar (left, from a daguerrotype made after their marriage in 1851). August was born in Germany, came to Wisconsin in his twenties and worked as a harness maker. Although he was a hard worker he found it difficult to support his large family as he moved from town to town, taking one job after another.

One summer day in 1869 when the Rüngelings were living in McGreggor, Iowa, a Mississippi river boat tied up at the town dock with Dan Rice's Great Pavillion Circus on board. The impoverished August must have thought himself fortunate that day when he was given a family pass to the show in exchange for a leather repair job he had done for one of the performers. That afternoon he took five of his sons to the circus. To them it was a glorious, unforgettable experience. Like most boys they had often played at circus in the back yard. But after seeing the Dan Rice show they began to play in earnest and made plans to start a real circus of their own.

Thirteen years after the Dan Rice show played in McGreggor the Ringling brothers (the name was now Anglicized) went on the road with a cast of eight (below). The "Fourth Season" on their poster (below, right) was stretching things a bit for it counted oldest brother Al's three previous years with small hall shows in which he had performed and sometimes managed. (Al was a strong man, tight wire and trapeze artist and juggler of no mean ability.) None of the other Ringling boys in the troupe—Otto, Alf T., Charles and John—had ever performed professionally. The little company toured the countryside for a season, came home to Baraboo and went out the next year as Ringling Brothers' Grand Carnival of Fun. Prominently billed in this show was youngest brother John (right), "The Emperor of Dutch Comedians," who offered "Dutch songs, positions, jokes, sayings, hibdy-dibdy fazes, and his roaring song and dance in Big Wooden Shoes."

FOURTH SEASON, 1882

RINGLING BROS.
CLASSIC AND COMIC CONCERT CO.

A REFINED AND HIGH-CLASS ENTERTAINMENT, CONTAINING MANY OF THE MOST PROMINENT FEATURES OF THE MUSICAL AND COMEDY WORLD

NEW FACES   NEW ACTS   NEW SONGS
NEW SAYINGS   NEW DANCES
WONDERFUL DANCERS   GREAT SPECIALISTS
NOTED COMEDIANS   FAMOUS SINGERS

TWO HOURS OF SOLID FUN
AN EVENING OF MELODY, MIRTH AND MERRIMENT
REFINED SOCIETY COMEDIES
CLASSICAL ORCHESTRA
UNIFORMED MILITARY BAND

Doors open at 7 p. m.   Performance begins at 8 p. m.
Popular prices of admission.

Grand Free Open-Air Concert and Parade every day at noon, and every evening at seven o'clock.

After two seasons the Ringlings had saved about $1,000 and with this money they financed their first circus. They were aided by "Yankee" Robinson (below), a well-known showman who had once owned a large circus but was now in poor shape and about to close.

Robinson lent his name to the new project and for a small fee was retained as adviser.

This photograph was taken about ten years after the brothers launched their first circus in Baraboo. Standing (left to right): Al, Alf T., Gus, Charles, Otto. Seated (l. to r.): John, Salome and August (parents), Ida (Mrs. Henry W. North) and Henry.

The five founding brothers whose faces appeared on the Ringling posters and programs were: Al, manager; Otto, treasurer; Alf T., publicity and concessions; Charles, advertising and advance; John, routing and advance. Henry acted as manager of other Ringling-owned shows. Gus was never an important factor although he was an advance man in the big show for eighteen years.

Right: John, the czar to be, as he looked in 1890.

The fabulous Ringling brothers were such a dedicated and efficient team that in ten years time they transformed their tiny show (as depicted here) into a huge, three-ring, 45-car railroad circus.

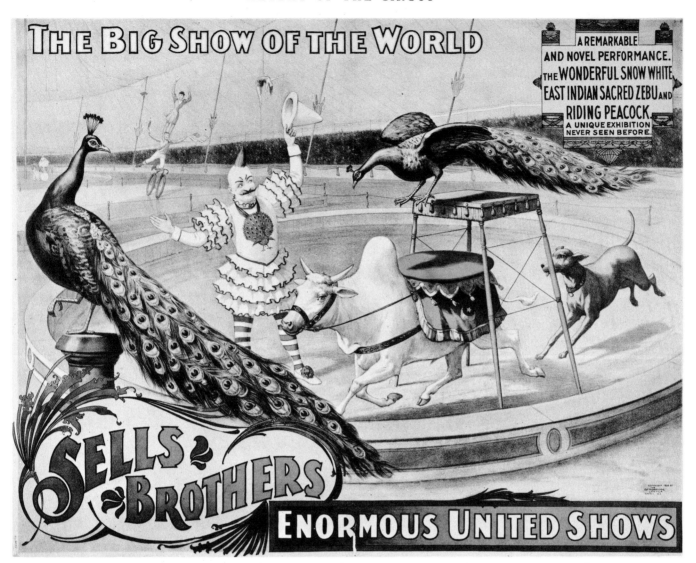

Among the many large shows competing against the upstart Ringlings in the eighties was the entrenched Sells Brothers Circus, which was twelve years old and traveling on rails when the Baraboo boys first went out under canvas. The four Sells brothers of Columbus, Ohio—like the Ringlings, a hard-working team—founded the show in 1872 and developed it into a first-rate circus of great size. In 1887 it boasted what is probably the longest title in circus history: "Sells Brothers' World Conquering and All-Overshadowing 3-Ring Circus, Real Roman Hippodrome, Grand Firemen's Tournament, Indian Village and Museum, Five Continent Menagerie and Pawnee Bill's Famous Original Wild West."

Featured by Sells was the famous clown, Billy Burke (right), father of actress Billie Burke.

Next to fire the thing most feared by showmen of the railroad era was a train wreck. The list of circus wrecks is a long one. Buffalo Bill and Barnum and Bailey, for instance, each suffered four damaging wrecks, John Robinson three, and so on. One disaster (shown in these photographs) took place on August 23, 1889, near Potsdam, New York, when several Barnum and Bailey stock cars telescoped.

Fortunately no one was killed in this wreck but thirty-one horses were destroyed, among them some valuable performing stallions and ring stock.

The worst wreck in circus history occurred at Ivanhoe, Indiana, on June 22, 1918, when an empty troop train plowed into four Hagenbeck Wallace sleeping cars, in which were some 260 people. Eighty-five were killed, 179 suffered injuries.

After the 1889 tour Barnum and Bailey shipped their show to England. The Jumbo incident had long been forgotten and Barnum (as the above British cartoon indicates) was greeted as an old friend.

153

THIS EVER-GROWING SHOW

IS NOW SO GREAT

NO BUILDING IN AMERICA CAN HOLD IT

Its Stage for "NERO" Requiring More Space
than an Entire City Block.

It Must Exhibit Always Under Canvas

—IN FAR BIGGER TENTS THAN EVER.—

And Its Investments and Daily Expenses have Increased so
Enormously that it Positively

During the winter of 1889-90 the enormous Barnum and Bailey show played at the Olympia in London (below). After a successful run three ocean liners brought the show back home that spring.

The aging Barnum (he was nearing eighty and had less than a year to live) announced that the circus was now so large that no building in America could hold it (above). He died on April 7, 1891.

W.W. COLE'S NEW 9 SHOWS CONSOLIDATED.

AERIEL.

AERIEL THE FLYING MAN WHO WITH HUGE ADJUSTABLE WINGS SOARS Through THE AIR AND RECEIVES $1,000 PER WEEK, WITH W.W.COLE'S GREAT SHOWS. Above the heads of the audience. The only LIVING HUMAN BEING who utilizes wings, as do the birds.

A great money-maker in the heyday of the circus was the W. W. Cole show which operated under various titles from 1871 to 1886. William Washington Cole (right), the founder and manager, was so reserved in manner and spoke so few words that he was nicknamed Chilly Billy. He was a genius in routing a show into new territory where money could be made. His 1873 show was the first to cross the continent entirely by rail. Later it went to Australia and New Zealand and returned to California. While not the largest circus, it was always popular and supplied the best acts, one of which was Aeriel (above) who soared about the tent on man-made wings.

A unique feature of the 1897 season was the Ringling mounted band, shown above lined up for a parade. From the time the Ringlings went on rails in 1890 the show was noted for its great bands and accomplished band directors. From a 25-piece band in 1891 the show reached a peak four years later with a 40-man band (it gave an hour's concert before every performance), plus a band of twenty-five in the big show and another of eleven in the side show.

On the left is H. Wells at the tiller of the Duryea horseless carriage, displayed by Barnum and Bailey in 1896. The wonderful new machine daily headed the parade and chugged around the hippodrome track before each performance. An editor wrote of it: "As it bumbles along, spasmodically coughing and belching noxious smoke, just ahead of the other freaks, it is obvious that the automobile has found its appropriate place."

THE GREAT AND ONLY TROUPE OF MARVELOUSLY EDUCATED SEA LIONS AND SEALS TRAINED BY CAPTAIN WOODWARD AND PERFORMED BY HIS TALENTED SONS. EVERY FEAT PICTURED ABOVE ACTUALLY PRESENTED AT EACH PERFORMANCE OR MONEY REFUNDED. $5000.00 WILL BE GIVEN TO ANY ONE PRODUCING A SIMILAR ACT. ALL OTHER SHOWS CLAIMING SUCH A FEATURE DO SO WILLFULLY AND WITH INTENT TO DEFRAUD THE PUBLIC.

Following the death of Adam Forepaugh in 1890 James A. Bailey became the owner of the show and in 1896 combined with the Sells brothers to put out a new circus under the title, Adam Forepaugh and Sells Brothers, with winter quarters in Columbus. One reason Bailey did this (he also bought into the Buffalo Bill show) was to furnish more competition for the rapidly growing Ringlings.

Featured in the new show along with its troupe of educated sea lions (above) was Madame Yucca (right), billed as "The Female Hercules, the Strongest Woman On Earth—Handsome, Modest and Genteel, In the Costume of the Parlor She Performs Feats of Strength Never Attempted By Any Other Man or Woman."

Forepaugh Sells stayed on the road through 1907, by which time the Ringlings had acquired full ownership.

Eight years after the Barnum and Bailey circus first went abroad it again crossed the Atlantic, this time to be away from home for five years (1897-1902). During its absence from America it made two winter stands in London, twice toured England, Scotland and Wales and then went on to Germany, France and several other European countries.

Above is an example of the show's active billing campaign in England. Below: A diagram of the lay-out at that time. The whole tour was an unprecedented success but not before Bailey solved many new problems. For instance, special railroad cars had to be built in England, and the height of the wagons reduced because of the low British tunnels.

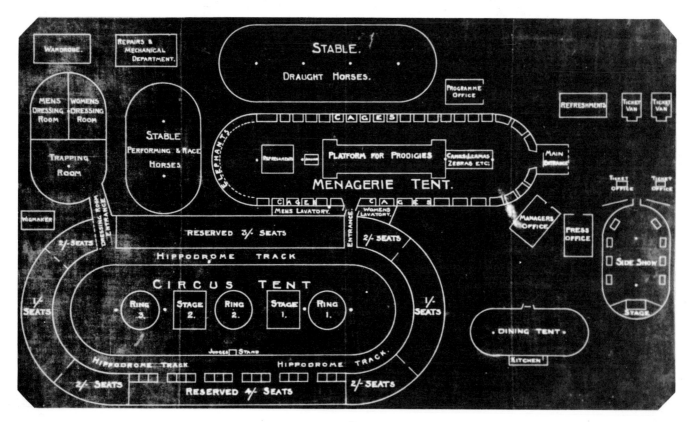

The original Siegrist-Silbon aerial troupe (above) starred in the show's European edition.

Below is the Barnum and Bailey 40-horse team of matched bays in Manchester, England, 1898.

The Greatest Show on Earth became *Die Grosste Schaustellung Der Erde* when the circus began its continental tour at Hamburg on April 15, 1900. Before the initial performance Hamburg saw the largest parade ever staged by Barnum and Bailey with the result that every seat was taken that afternoon although it was Easter Sunday. After four weeks in Hamburg the show moved to Berlin where it gave twenty-eight performances. In that city the circus was closely observed by officers of the German General Staff who were interested not in the performances but in the organization and the clocklike manner in which the show was put up and taken down. Some methods used by the circus were later adopted by the German Army. In the winter of 1900-01 the show was quartered in Vienna.

By the time the show reached Germany the freaks were no longer billed as such but had become "prodigies." This came about in England when the freaks met in assembly and decided that the word "freak" should be abolished and a less offensive one substituted. The London press got hold of the story and devoted columns to the "Uprising of the Freaks." Hundreds of letters poured in suggesting a new name. The one finally selected was submitted by Canon Wilberforce of Westminster Abbey. Thus did the freaks become prodigies—but not for long. In 1903 when the circus reopened in the United States, the banners, as usual, read "Hall of Freaks."

The photographs on the opposite page show (above) one of the English-built railroad cars at the Hamburg dock and (below) the arrival in Paris.

The tableau wagon "America" was one of a series of wagons Bailey had built for his 1903 homecoming.

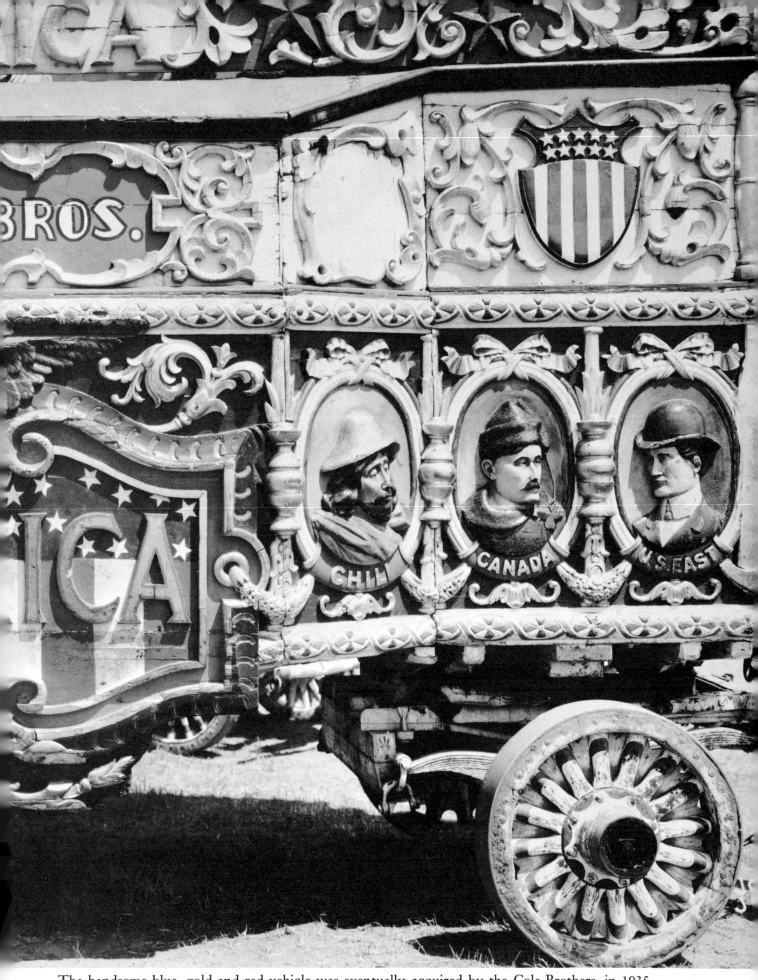

The handsome blue, gold and red vehicle was eventually acquired by the Cole Brothers, in 1935.

America got its first look at Barnum and Bailey's great 40-horse team in 1903. These two views show how it looked from the sidelines (above, pulling the "Two Hemispheres" bandwagon) and from the driver's seat (left). The team paraded in this country in 1903 and 1904 and was usually driven by Jim Thomas who had two helpers at his side. One man worked the wheel brakes, the other kept the reins straight and took in the slack. Thomas, sitting eighty feet behind the four-abreast lead horses, held ten reins in each hand—one for each two horses.

The 40-horse hitch was nothing new in America. It had been used before by Spalding and Rogers in 1848, by Yankee Robinson in 1866 and by the Dan Rice Circus in 1873.

Despite Bailey's triumphant return and the great parades he staged he was no longer supreme, for the Ringlings were now his equal in size.

Although the two circus giants—Barnum & Bailey and the Ringlings—had the spotlight, there were numerous little "dog and pony" shows at that time which were in great favor in rural America.

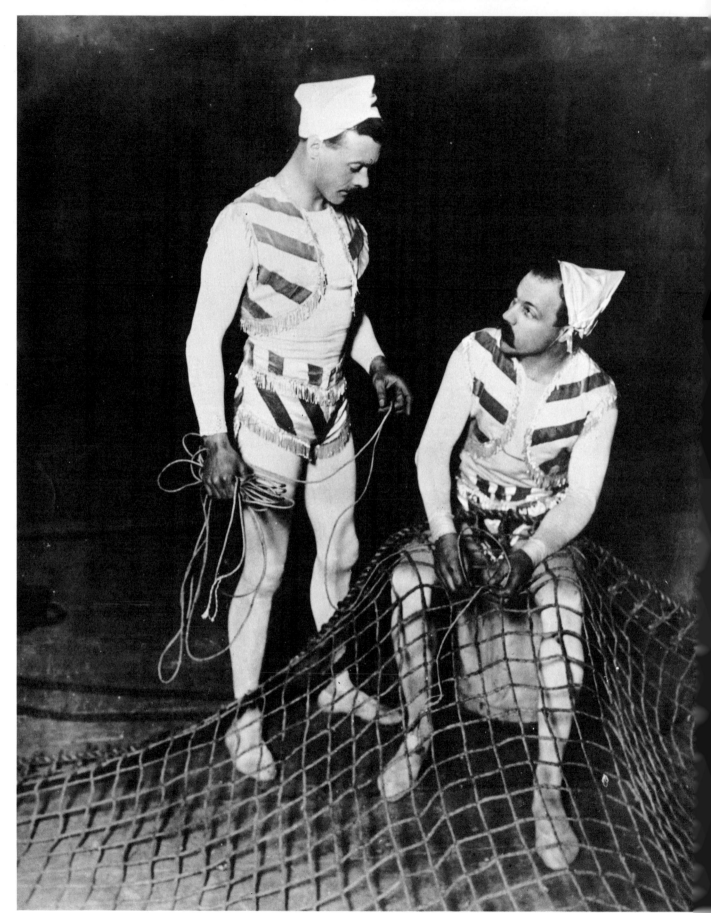

On these two pages are shown some of the noted performers of the Ringling and Barnum and Bailey shows. (The Ringlings bought control of the older circus in 1907, a year after the death of James A. Bailey, but the shows operated independently until 1919 when they combined under the present title.)

Opposite page: Charles and Ernest Clarke, the great English acrialists who made their American debut with Barnum and Bailey in 1903. One of the most versatile of all flyers, Ernest was the first to do a double somersault to a catch with a full pirouette added, the first to regularly do the triple. The superb brother team was a Ringling headline feature from 1906 to 1926.

On the right is Frank (Slivers) Oakley in his lobster riding act. A master of pantomime, Oakley's specialty was his one-man baseball game. He was the most popular buffoon of his time. Slivers always worked alone and earned up to $750 a week.

Below: Members of the Davenport family, an American troupe of outstanding accomplishment.

This photograph of the Campbell Brothers Circus parade (
across the strip to the right then across the second strip and so

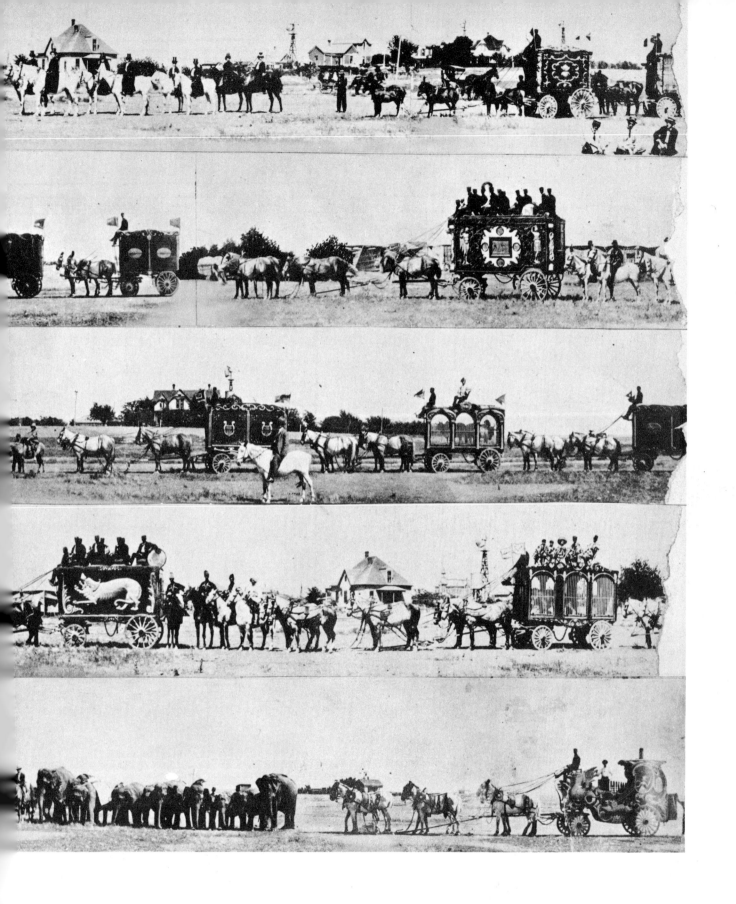

in 1908) starts at the top left with the escort wagon, goes
n to the calliope (lower right) at the end of the procession.

ZAZEL

THE DAREDEVILS

Common to all large shows during the heyday of the circus was the "death-defying stunt," a type of thriller now almost extinct. Many of these acts involved an apparatus, such as the one used in the 1870's by the daring Lulu, pioneer of the mechanical thrill act. Lulu, a man made up to look like a girl, stood on a small plate flush with the stage floor beneath which were strong springs. At a signal the springs were released and up shot Lulu to a distance of thirty feet, where he grasped a trapeze.

Lulu's feat was the forerunner of the cannon act, first performed in this country in 1879 by George Loyal, the "Human Projectile." Following him came Zazel, an English girl named Rosa M. Richter, who was "fired bodily from a cannon, flying with violent velocity through the air for a distance of over 75 feet and falling upon a net." Zazel in pink tights climbed into the mouth of the wooden cannon and at the instant of her release (by a powerful spring) a charge of gunpowder was set off—a technique which remains basically unchanged today. Zazel was featured in various circuses, as were other Zazels who borrowed the name of the English girl.

One of the earliest bicycle thrill acts was performed by Leonati, a Frenchman billed on the Forepaugh show in 1883 as the "Spiral Ascensionist."

On a high wheeler (it was before the day of the pneumatic safety bike) Leonati rode to a 50-foot high platform and then descended to the ground.

M'lle ELLA ZUILA
AERIAL QUEEN,
RIDING HER VELOCIPEDE
Over a 3-4 Inch Wire,
100 FEET IN MID-AIR

ONLY TO BE SEEN IN
THE GREAT
Forepaugh Show
200 Exhibitions at Crystal Palace,
London (Eng.), and the
LEADING CITIES OF EUROPE

THE WORLD'S LAST AND GREATEST WONDER

The laws of gravitation defied by

ZUILA, THE FEMALE BLONDIN

Impossibilities accomplished ; she

RIDES A VELOCIPEDE OVER A 3-4 INCH WIRE, 100 FEET IN MID-AIR.

This daring, youthful little French woman accomplishes the wonderful and never before attempted feat of

Riding upon a Bicycle, Backward and Forward, over a High Wire

100 FEET ABOVE THE HEADS of ten thousand spectators, maintaining, during the perilous performance, a perfectly easy and graceful position, and traversing the lofty line with all the celerity and skill that the most accomplished bicyclist displays upon the smoothly paved boulevard or level floor. This astounding, startling

DANGER-DEFYING VELOCIPEDE RACE ON THE AERIAL ROADWAY

MLLE D'ZIZI

SPANNING DEATH'S ARCH AWHEEL—
FEARFUL, FLYING, FRENZIED, FLIGHT
ACROSS A FRIGHTFUL ABYSS 55 FEET WIDE.
THE BRAVEST HEART CEASES TO BEAT
WHILE THIS INTREPID DAUGHTER OF
FRANCE SOARS TOWARDS THE HEAVENS.

DARE DEVIL RIDE ABOVE A YAWNING DEATH ARCH

Chasm Vaulting Event of Supernatural Sensation. Terrific, Towering, Soaring Head long Action, challenging the Omnipotence and Omnipresence of accepted natural law

SCIENTISTS DAZZLED. THE PUBLIC PUZZLED.

A Transcendently Amazing and Electrifying New Feature

ABSOLUTELY FREE TO ALL

WHO VISIT OUR SHOW GROUNDS IMMEDIATELY AFTER THE PARADE AND AGAIN AT 6·30 P. M.

Too Expensive for any other shows to have, The Great

WALTER L. MAIN'S   AMERICA'S BEST   SHOWS

Now present this Incomprehensible, Seemingly Superhuman Triumph over Nature Twice Daily in the Open Air and which you can witness without paying one cent of Admission.

GREATEST AND MOST EXCITING GRATUITOUS EXHIBITION EVER EXPLOITED

One of the most daring of the high wire performers was Ella Zuila, shown on the opposite page riding her wooden bicycle on a 100-foot high wire (from a Forepaugh courier, 1881). A versatile artiste, Zuila offered an assortment of stunts. She walked with her feet encased in baskets, on iron stilts, with her head and body enveloped in a sack, carried her husband on her shoulders, trundled her child in a wheelbarrow and poured water over her head in an arc from one vase to another.

Above: Mlle. D'Zizi who thrilled crowds in 1899 by leaping a gap on her bike over six elephants.

When the safety bike was introduced in the nineties audiences were soon treated to a number of neck-risking acts, some of which are shown on these pages. The simplest was the straightaway speed act (above), as performed by Starr in the Forepaugh Sells show, 1903. Starr shot down a ladder with such terrific speed that the momentum carried him all the way around the hippodrome track.

Left: Minting, the "Australian Marvel," who rode a unicycle on a 20-inch wide spiral roadway to the summit, sixty feet high, and then descended. Forepaugh Sells billed him in 1902 as the "Only Unicycle Ascensionist in the World."

More sensational was the Loop the Loop as performed by Diavolo (opposite page, above) in 1904. One of the first to do this dangerous stunt, Diavolo sped down a long incline which turned a complete loop causing him to perform a somersault at great speed. Casualties ran high among the Loop the Loopers.

The picture beneath shows Prodigious Porthos in his 50-foot flight (Forepaugh Sells, 1904).

WHEN—EXACTLY AS ABOVE PHOTOGRAPHICALLY PORTRAYED, AND PRECISELY AS IT WILL BE PRESENTED HERE—WE INTRODUCED THE ABOVE INCREDIBLY DIFFICULT, DEXTEROUS AND FAR MORE THAN OUTDARING DEVIL-DARE ACHIEVEMENT, IN MADISON SQUARE GARDEN, NEW YORK CITY, IT CREATED A SENSATION ALMOST AS INDESCRIBABLE AS IS ITSELF. IT DEPOPULATED OTHER PLACES OF AMUSEMENT. THE METROPOLITAN PRESS DEVOTED WHOLE PAGES TO PICTURING AND PRAISING IT. IT WAS THE CHIEF TOPIC ON EVERY TONGUE, FROM THE BATTERY TO FAR BEYOND THE BRONX. ITS WELL-NIGH AWFUL AUDACITY FAIRLY STUNNED THE HUNDREDS OF THOUSANDS WHO MANAGED TO GET IN AHEAD OF THE COUNTLESS THRONGS VAINLY CLAMORING TO SEE IT, AND EVERYWHERE IT WAS THE SAME. WHAT MORE IS THERE TO SAY THAN THAT WE ALONE EXHIBIT IT?

THIS SEASON IS ALSO STRENUOUSLY SIGNALIZED BY THE FIRST APPEARANCE IN AMERICA, AND WITH OUR UNITED CIRCUSES ONLY, OF DIAVOLO'S ONLY RIVAL IN DESPERATE DEEDS AWHEEL—"THE CHASM-VAULTING CYCLIST," WHO ALSO, AT EACH PERFORMANCE, IS ACTUALLY SEEN COMPLETING A SEEMINGLY FATAL AND APPALLINGLY INTERRUPTED TRIP ON HIS BIKE, BY MIRACULOUSLY EXE-CUTING A MID-AIR, HAIR-RAISING, HEART-HALTING, FIFTY-FOOT FLIGHT, HIGH IN SPACE, AND LANDING SAFELY AND COMPOSEDLY ON THE FURTHER SIDE, JUST AS ABOVE TRUTHFULLY AND ACCURATELY ILLUSTRATED. ON THE 23d OF JANUARY LAST, THE NEW YORK AMERICAN AND JOURNAL PAID THIS ACT THE UNPRECEDENTEDLY HIGH COMPLIMENT OF PUBLISHING, WITH A PICTURE, A SPECIAL CABLEGRAM FROM LONDON, DESCRIBING IT, AND WHICH IT WELL DESERVED.

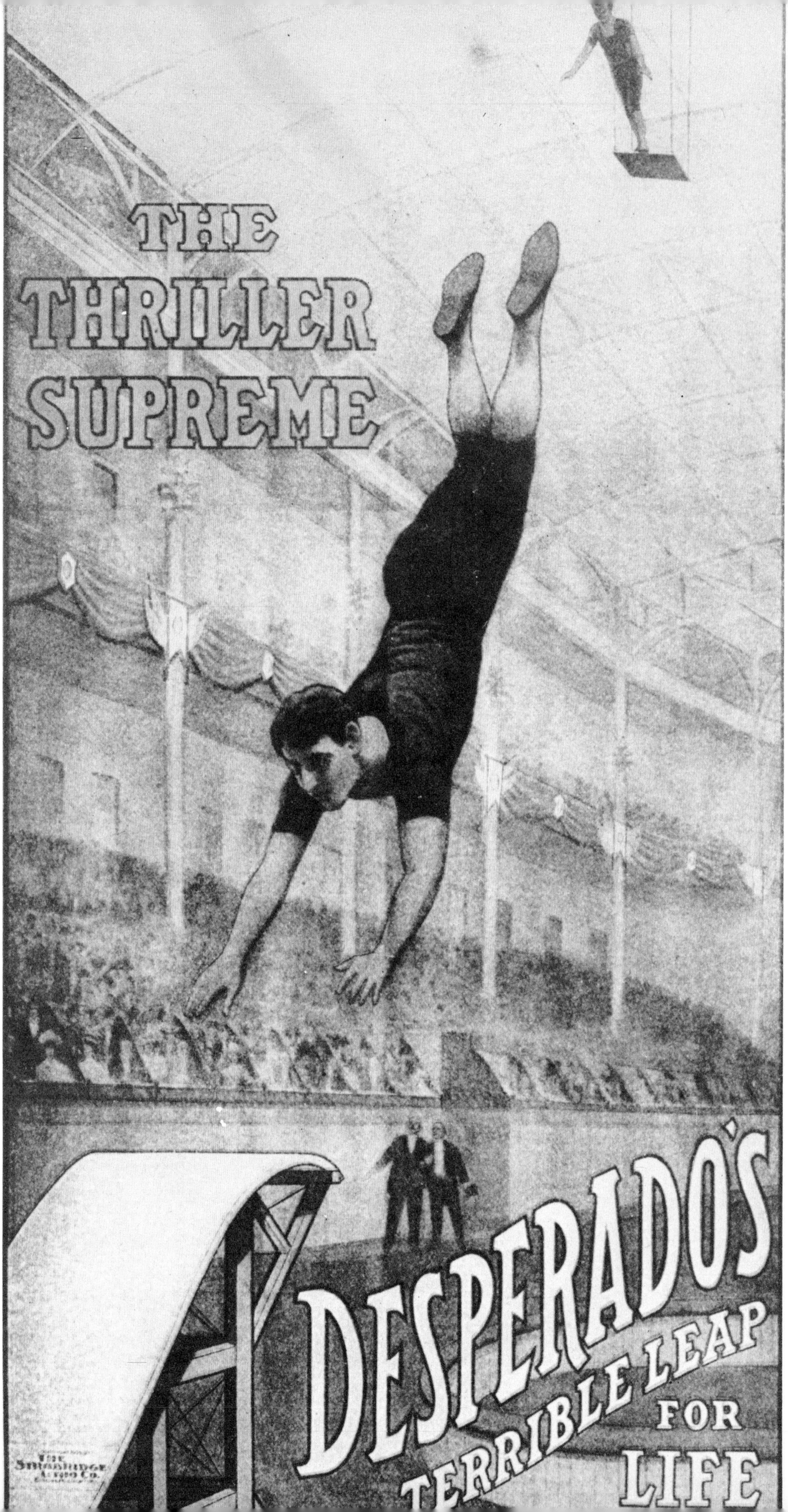
THE
THRILLER
SUPREME
DESPERADO'S
TERRIBLE LEAP
FOR
LIFE

Ernest Gadbin, a German acrobat of matchless nerve who performed for Barnum and Bailey just before the first world war, was perhaps the greatest of all the daredevils. Billed as Desperado (opposite page), he did a swan dive from an 80-foot-high platform and landed on his chest on an inclined wooden slide which was highly polished and sprinkled with a thin layer of corn meal. At the moment of contact his speed was better than 100 feet per second. The slide was upturned at both ends and Desperado would skid down and up it and then shoot off into space to land in a net.

Desperado was the originator of this unique and dangerous stunt. He had many imitators but none dared try it without the use of protective padding to cushion the shock of landing on the slide. Desperado stood alone in his field.

About this time Barnum and Bailey introduced a hair-raiser called L'auto Bolide or the Dip of Death (below). The daring rider was Isabella Butler, a "handsome, beautifully-gowned American girl," according to the 1907 program. Miss Butler was strapped in the seat of the primitive auto which started its run from a high platform. In response to the director's signal came her reply, "All ready, sir," and there was never a "quiver in the musical voice." The car ran down a steep incline, turned upside down and, still inverted, shot "into space forty feet away across a veritable chasm of death," then landed on the other incline, righted itself and finished its wild run on the track.

Desperado and Miss Butler marked the end of an era. With their passing the daredevil and mechanical thrill acts began to fade out.

THE SPECTACLE

Gone with the daredevils is the old-time Spectacle, an elaborate production of DeMille proportions once used as an opener by all the large circuses.

The old 'Spec' bore little resemblance to its modern offspring, which is often called a Spec but is generally not much more than a costumed walkaround with a few flourishes added.

The true Spec was a play, a pageant-like performance of staggering size. It had a plot and told a story and consumed up to half an hour of a show's running time. It had a cast of principals, scenery and stage effects and it depicted in song, dialogue and action stories from the Bible and Mythology, historical events and Fairyland tales. It employed almost everyone in the show including bandsmen, roustabouts, clowns, most of the animals and often used professional actors for the important talking roles.

Circuses tried to outdo each other in presenting these lavish pageants. Some of the grander ones were: "Solomon and the Queen of Sheba," "Nero or the Burning of Rome," "Jerusalem and the Crusades," "Cleopatra," "Joan of Arc," and "Cinderella" (right), produced by Ringling Brothers in 1916.

Here, on a stage with scenery, Cinderella is shown losing her slipper as she dashes down the stairs while the clock strikes twelve. To stage this Spec the Ringlings used a cast of 1,370 (including 60 clowns), 735 horses and "five herd of elephants." It was, said the Ringling program, "the longest, costliest and most magnificent processional triumphant ever presented anywhere."

The old Spec, despite its magnificence, was a rather slow-moving, top-heavy affair, which is probably the reason it has vanished from the circus scene.

RINGL
THE MAGNIFICENT FA

TWO COMPLETE CIRCUS PERFORMANCES DAILY AT 2 &
8 P.M. DOORS OPEN AT 1 AND 7 P.M ONE SINGLE ADMISSION TICKE
ADMITS TO EVERYTHING
INCLUDING THE SPECTACLE
CHILDREN UNDER 12 YEARS HALF PRICE

NG BROS
LATEST AND GREATEST FEATURE
LAND SPECTACLE CINDERELLA
AT 10 A.M. PRECEDING THE FIRST PERFORMANCE
LONGEST COSTLIEST AND MOST GORGEOUS
FREE STREET PARADE
EVER SEEN IN THIS OR ANY OTHER COUNTRY

"Cleopatra," an earlier Spec, was presented by Barnum and Bailey in 1895. (The above scene shows a slave smuggling Cleopatra into the Palace.) The cast of 1,250 included 300 dancing girls, 500 mounted Roman soldiers, 200 foot soldiers, 22 principal actors, "noble ladies, slaves, captives, prophets, scribes, etc.," and the entire menagerie.

The Specs used all available animals whether or not they properly fitted into the theme depicted. For example in the "Joan of Arc" Spec (opposite page) forty elephants were used. It is doubtful if the real Joan ever saw an elephant but Ringling's Joan certainly did during the 1913 season. Her army was further bolstered by 650 mounted soldiers.

One of the last of the big railroad Wild West shows was the 101 Ranch which reigned from 1908 to 1931, less eight years when it was off the road. Organized by the Miller brothers of Oklahoma (Joseph, Zack and George), it was at first a straight Wild West show, later became more circus-like.

The pictures on this page illustrate the change in the show's character. Left: The 1910 show which was purely western and (above) the 1928 presentation, featuring the incongruous "Julius Caesar" Spec. In its initial stage it was a good money-maker, netting its owners $800,000 until it closed in 1917 at the government's request. (The Millers' 110,000-acre ranch was used during the war to supply the Army with horses and mules.) Reorganized in 1925, the show was never again successful.

Buffalo Bill finished his career with this show. The old hero had lost his own show (in 1913), performed for Sells Floto and in 1916 went with the 101 Ranch. He gave his last performance on November 11, 1916 and died two months later.

The above photograph, taken in Madison Square Garden, New York, in 1910, shows the clown wedding of Barnum and Bailey's Harry La Pearl and Mable McGinley. La Pearl was the show's most popular buffoon for many years, provoking much laughter with his "Suffragettes' Meeting" act and clown band.

At the turn of the century the Millettes (right) amazed audiences with a stunt that has yet to be duplicated—the forward *double* somersault from shoulder to shoulder without any mechanical aid. It involved three men: two understanders (pitcher and catcher) who stood about twelve feet apart, and the leaper, Ernest Schlee (far right in the photo). Schlee would stand on the pitcher's shoulders and at a signal the two would crouch and push off simultaneously. In the air Schlee would turn two complete somersaults and land on his feet on the catcher's shoulders. This was only one of several stunts the Millettes (later a five-man team) originated and perfected.

The Living Statues, a relic of the nineties, were a delight to the ladies and some men but a never failing bore to all small boys who must have been glad when the display was discontinued in 1935.

The gilded or whitened figures posed motionless in a series of tableaux that depicted such subjects as "The Dance of Life," "Victory," "The Spirit of Flight," and "The Rainbow Fountain."

185

5 The BIG ONE and Others

When the Ringling Brothers bought control of Barnum and Bailey in the summer of 1907 (for the bargain price of $410,000) the star equestrienne of the older circus was Ella Bradna (above, right) who had been performing in the center ring for two seasons with an Englishman named Derrick, an acrobatic rider of great skill. Ella's husband was Fred Bradna (above, in the role of equestrian director), who was born Frederick Ferber but assumed his wife's more famous name.

The story of the Bradna couple goes back to its romantic beginnings in the spring of 1901, when Fred, a young Cavalry officer in the German Army, attended a performance of the *Nouveau Cirque* in Paris and saw the debut of his future wife from a ringside box. At the end of her act the horse suddenly shied and Ella was tossed over the ringbank into Fred's arms. This was their first meeting.

Before he left the arena that evening Fred made two decisions. He would marry the lovely equestrienne, and he would join the circus. Both came to pass. The marriage took place in 1903 and the couple came to America to open with Barnum and Bailey—Ella as an established star, Fred as her assistant and horseman.

For more than forty years the Bradnas trouped with the circus, with Barnum and Bailey and with the Big One, as the enormous show was called when the two great circuses merged in 1919 to become Ringling Brothers and Barnum & Bailey.

Ella enjoyed twenty-nine consecutive seasons of center ring stardom. Her husband rose to the important position of equestrian director (stage manager) and in that capacity knew and worked with every performer of note during his long career. Some of them are shown on the following pages.

The Hanneford Riding Troupe, headed by the great equestrian clown, Edwin (Poodles) Hanneford (right), came to this country from England in 1915 and members of it have been riding ever since.

Poodles, clad in a long coonskin coat and carrying a huge walking stick, delighted audiences for years with his assumed awkwardness, fake falls and other antics. His act was a modernization of the old "Pete Jenkins" routine (originated by Charles Sherwood in the 1850's) in which a trick rider in the guise of a drunk staggers into the ring, clings clumsily to a horse, then sheds a series of coats and pants, eventually emerging in tights to give a finished performance.

The Hanneford Troupe was with the Big One for fifteen seasons and starred in several other shows.

Below (from left to right): Percy Clarke, Grace (Mrs. Poodles) Hanneford, Poodles, his mother Nana, his sister, Elizabeth Hanneford Clarke, and her husband, Ernest Clarke. Photo was taken in 1931.

MAY WIRTH
WORLD FAMOUS EQUESTRIENNE
THE GREATEST BARE-BACK RIDER THAT EVER LIVED

MAY WIRTH Somersaulting From The Back Of One Galloping Horse To Another! Jumping From The Ground To Her Flying Steed **WITH BASKETS ON HER FEET!**

In 1912 a sixteen-year-old Australian girl named May Wirth made her debut in Madison Square Garden on the Barnum and Bailey circus and was immediately acclaimed as the finest equestrienne in the world.

"Pretty of face and finely formed, she is the acme of ease and grace," stated the *New York Clipper*'s critic. "But she does not rely upon her physical attractions for her success. She is an equestrienne in all that the word implies."

There is no doubt that May Wirth was the greatest woman bareback rider the world has ever seen. She did with ease things that few men and no women could do—the forward somersault, the back backward (as James Robinson did it, with his back toward the horse's head), and she could somersault from one horse to another. More than that the Australian beauty was a showman of the first order. "Her like will never be seen again," wrote Fred Bradna.

Bird Millman was the first American wire artiste to perform without the aid of a balancing umbrella. A favorite of the 1920's, the dainty and vivacious performer sang solos as she danced the wire.

The twenties have often been called the Golden Age of the circus because of the outstanding stars it produced, and the most illustrious of all—of that or any other era—was Lillian Leitzel, queen of the aerialists for twelve years on the Big One.

She was under five feet tall, weighed less than 100 pounds and her overdeveloped shoulders and arms gave her an almost gnomelike appearance. She was not beautiful by any standard but her act was overpowering. She opened it by climbing a rope (or web, in circus parlance) in a series of "rollups" to a pair of Roman rings which were suspended just below the peak of the tent. With no net beneath she twirled about in effortless grace for several minutes and then descended to the center ring.

Now came the second half of her act. This time she was pulled aloft on a rope and, placing her right hand and wrist in a loop attached to a swivel, she began a series of revolutions known as the plange turn. She would keep herself going in a continuous circle, literally throwing her body over her own shoulder to pivot. As the drums rolled and the crowd took up the count she would repeat the turns about 100 times. (She once performed this difficult and dangerous feat 239 times without stopping.) Leitzel's plange turn was not as graceful as her work on the Roman rings. It was a test of stamina but it had great crowd appeal and made her so famous that she demanded and got a private car on the circus train. She was the only performer to be so honored.

Alfredo Codona, a handsome Mexican-born flyer of incomparable grace, was the show's male star and almost the equal of Leitzel in drawing power. Inevitably the two became attached to each other, and in July, 1928, they were married (left).

Connoisseurs of flying trapeze acts unanimously agree that Codona was the supreme perfectionist in technique, the most brilliant stylist of all time. Other flyers have done what Codona did—the double somersault, the two-and-a-half, the triple and the double pirouette while returning from the catcher's hands to the trapeze (Codona was caught by his brother, Lalo) but none has ever been able to approach him in form. It was flawless.

Opposite page: Codona lightly clasps the swing bar.

On Friday, February 13, 1931, in Copenhagen, Denmark, Lillian Leitzel fell to the floor and died two days later. (The above illustration of her final flight from earth with the death-causing broken swivel on her wrist was painted by Hugo Zacchini.)

Less than two years after her death Codona married Vera Bruce, an aerialist. Soon afterwards he had a bad fall which ended his career. In 1937 while discussing divorce with his wife in a law office he shot her to death, then killed himself.

Hugo Zacchini (above), painter and human projectile, revived the old cannonball act in 1929 with a monster machine that gave off a deafening blast and shot him (by compressed air) some seventy feet up into the air for a lateral distance of 135 feet at an initial speed of eighty miles per hour. The new cannon, valued at $35,000, was developed in Italy by Hugo's father, Ildebrano.

Hugo was heavily featured on the Big One in 1929 and again in 1934, when he and his brother Victoria, were simultaneously shot from the cannon.

There have been several women animal trainers in the history of the circus but none could compare with Mable Stark, a graduate nurse who gave up her cap in 1911 when she joined the Al G. Barnes show. A good looking blonde, Miss Stark is the only woman who has broken, trained and worked tigers, and taught them to wrestle with her (as above). This was her speciality—an on-the-ground, rollover wrestling bout with a full-grown Bengal. She finished the sensational act by putting her face in the tiger's mouth. She was always unarmed, working without a gun, whip, iron fork or chair. At one time she had sixteen tigers in the cage, probably the largest number ever handled by any trainer. During her career she was mauled and bitten many times.

Left: One of her young tigers takes a slash at a visitor to her training quarters.

In 1914 Emil Pallenberg, a German bear trainer, arrived in this country to be featured with his wife, Catherine, on the Ringling show. Working with Russian bears on a platform without a cage, the Pallenbergs showed audiences something brand new —bears that could roller skate and ride bicycles.

The Pallenbergs originated many tricks that have since become standard. During the first world war when foreign talent was scarce they commanded the highest salary on the show. They were with Ringling and the Big One for thirteen consecutive years and at one time owned three other bear acts.

The greatest circus bandmaster of modern times is Merle Evans (above, with the Big One's 1955 band) who mounted the Ringling bandstand in 1919 and except for part of one season when he was forced to join a musician's strike, did not miss a single performance until he left the show in mid-season, 1955, following a disagreement with John Ringling North. During that 37-year period he led the band more than 18,000 times without missing an important cue. This is a remarkable achievement when it is considered that a single act may involve some twenty quick cue changes and that the bands Evans led played snatches from over 200 different pieces every performance, including marches, waltzes and rumbas.

On the left is a Ringling-Barnum clown band of the 1920's, one that Evans did *not* lead.

In this characteristic pose Evans faces the arena with his back to the musicians and conducts them with his left hand while tooting the cornet. Evans has said that his most difficult job was accompanying dancing horses, for the animals do not follow the music, as it appears. The band follows *them*.

In the twenties the durable windjammer directed a band averaging thirty-six pieces but after the death of Charles Ringling, a devotee of music, the number was gradually reduced. In his last season he had twenty-six men. In 1956 violins were used in the band, to the horror of all circus lovers.

The supreme tight wire artist was Con Colleano (opposite page), of Spanish-Irish ancestry, who came to this country in the twenties from his native Australia and was a favorite for many seasons on the Big One and other shows. In the costume of a toreador Colleano danced the bolero in flashing style, threw a backward somersault and removed his trousers in the air as he turned. His great stunt, however, was the perilous feet-to-feet forward somersault which he alone could do. Although this feat has since been duplicated, Colleano originated it. (It is far more difficult than the "backward," for in the "forward" the legs are in front of the eyes during the turn and the performer cannot see the wire before he alights.)

Colleano's sister, Winnie (above) thrilled audiences with her heel-and-toe performance on the high trapeze. Her climactic stunt was to swing on the bar in a sitting position and then let go completely and catch herself by the heels. She did not attempt the difficult feat until she had spent nearly twenty years on the trapeze.

Ala Naitto (right, on the shoulders of her sister, Nio) is known as the "female Colleano," for she is the only woman who has accomplished the forward somersault on the wire. In addition to juggling hoops in this manner she could do a head stand on her sister's head while Nio went up a flight of steps, walked the thin wire and came down the steps on the other side.

In 1926 Charles Ringling died and John was the only one left of the seven brothers. A millionaire many times over, John that year completed in Sarasota, Florida, the enormous mansion *Ca' d' Zan* (House of John) at a cost of about one million dollars with an additional $250,000 for the seawall, swimming pool and other buildings on the grounds. The total effect was a Dodge's Venetian Palace, Madison Square Garden and the big top.

About that time the American Circus Corporation, a syndicate headed by Jeremiah Mugivan, owned five major circuses which the group offered to sell to John Ringling. The offer was not taken seriously at first but when Mugivan announced in 1929 that the syndicate's Sells Floto show was scheduled to open in the Garden that spring, thus freezing out the Big One, Ringling bought the entire corporation.

He was now the absolute circus king but he had made a costly deal. He had to borrow heavily to finance it and disaster was in store for him.

This photograph of John Ringling was taken in 1930 when he held title to every circus of consequence in the United States. Below: his yacht which often brought New Yorkers to Sarasota.

John's first wife, Mable (above, as she looked in 1905), who planned the ornate mansion in detail, died only three years after it was completed. The residence is now owned by the State of Florida.

CIRCUS COMING

The advance billing a circus received before its arrival in a town was—and still is, for that matter—of vital importance to its success. In the railroad era a show was preceded by a banner brigade—men who traveled on regular trains and tacked cloth banners on the sides of buildings. They were followed by the number one advertising car with a crew of some thirty billposters and lithographers who daubed about everything standing within a range of 100 miles from the place of exhibition. With them came the show's press agents to handle the editorial end in the local newspapers. The number two advertising car followed with more billposters, lithographers, programmers and press agents. After them came the 24-hour men to check the lot, the contracts, the licenses and to see that the billing was in good order.

The assorted posters on the opposite page would indicate that there were many circuses that ignored Ringling's claim to be the Greatest Show On Earth.

LEWIS BROS 3 RING CIRCUS LARGEST SHOW IN THE WORLD!!

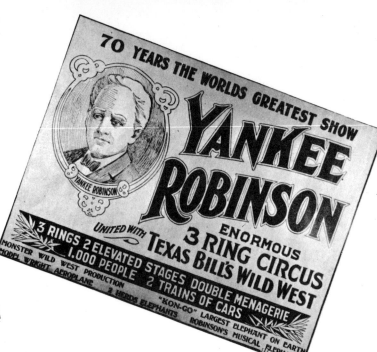

70 YEARS THE WORLDS GREATEST SHOW
YANKEE ROBINSON
ENORMOUS 3 RING CIRCUS
UNITED WITH Texas Bill's WILD WEST
3 RINGS 2 ELEVATED STAGES DOUBLE MENAGERIE
1.000 PEOPLE 2 TRAINS OF CARS
MONSTER WILD WEST PRODUCTION
MODEL WRIGHT AEROPLANE
2 HERDS ELEPHANTS "KON-GO" LARGEST ELEPHANT ON EARTH
ROBINSON'S MUSICAL ELEPHANTS

WIRTH BROS.
GREATEST
SHOW ON EARTH

COOK BROS.
WORLD'S GREATEST SHOWS INC.
AMERICA'S NEWEST AND MIGHTIEST AMUSEMENT MARVEL
Cook Bros. Zoological Exhibition Finest in the Entire World

ATTERBURY TRAINED ANIMAL SHOW
LARGEST SHOW IN THE WORLD

This sequence of photographs shows the execution of Black Diamond, an Al G. Barnes tusker. The beast went berserk in Corsicana, Texas, on October 12, 1929, crushed a woman to death, wrecked an auto and injured two trainers. John Ringling, recent purchaser of the show, wired, "Kill Diamond in some humane way." The elephant was led to a clearing in the woods (below).

He was chained to three trees while five marksmen armed with high-powered rifles stood about six yards away. The first volley struck Diamond behind the ears and he looked inquiringly around. He completely ignored the second volley but at the third he started suddenly and then went down. The men continued to pump lead into him from all angles. It took more than fifty bullets to finish him off.

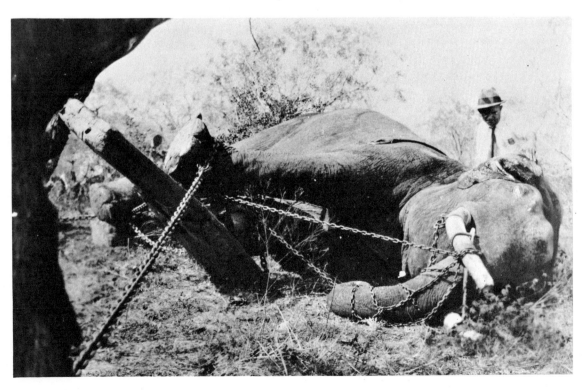

The most spine-chilling act within memory is the pyramid high wire display of the Wallendas, who received a show-stopping ovation of fifteen minutes at their debut on the Big One in 1928. Since then the original troupe (left, Herman, Joe, Carl and Helen) has increased in size, as has their act—from two-high to three-high with as many as nine performers on the wire at the same time.

Working some forty feet aloft mostly without a net, the reckless Wallendas move across the wire on bicycles or walk it in a tableau display with a chair at the peak. The troupe has had some bad spills. At a matinee in Akron, Ohio, in 1934, the wire suddenly sagged and threw the quartet off balance. All the equipment crashed down. Carl grabbed the wire and caught Helen by the neck with his legs as she fell past. He held her until a portable net was brought out and they dropped safely. Meantime Herman with a similar hold on Joseph, went hand over hand on the wire to the platform with his brother dangling below. No one was injured.

Clyde Beatty, billed as "the youngest and most fearless wild animal trainer," made his Ringling debut in 1931 but he appeared only during the New York and Boston stands and did not go on the road.

The 27-year old Beatty, using whip, chair, revolver and theatrics on his lions and tigers was the first trainer used by the Big One since 1926, when John Ringling decided to abolish wild animal acts.

Featured with the Wallendas on the 1928 show was the three-and-a-quarter-ton sea elephant, Goliath.

The monster ate 150 pounds of fish every day and was transported on a private railroad stock car.

The greatest side-show attraction ever promoted by the Big One was the Ubangi group of thirteen saucer-lipped women and two men who traveled with the show in 1930 and again in 1932. They were paid $1,500 a week but most of the money went to their exploiter, Dr. Ludwig Bergonnier, who had brought them out of French West Africa.

The Ubangis gauge the beauty of their women by the length of their lips. By that standard Queen Guetika (right) was the loveliest of all.

The enlargement is accomplished by inserting small disks in the slit lips of infants and increasing the size of the disks as the girls grow.

The Ubangis were a tremendous gate attraction, though foul-smelling and savage. They gobbled down raw fish and unpeeled bananas. One of them fell in love with Merle Evans but he was not interested.

Who was the greatest flyer of all time—Ernest Clarke, Alfredo Codona, or the more recent master of the triple somersault, Arthur Concello? The question provokes argument whenever circus people gather but there is never any question when it comes to naming the greatest woman flyer. She was Antoinette Concello, shown in the above photograph standing between catcher Eddie Ward, Jr. (on the left) and her husband, Art. Antoinette was the first and only woman to achieve the triple and the act in which she performed it (The Flying Con-

cellos) stands above all others, for it is the only one that ever had two triple somersaulters on the same bill.

In 1933 when Codona injured his shoulder the Concellos replaced him in the center ring. About that time Antoinette was doing the two-and-a-half and before long she had graduate to the ultimate—the triple.

The picture on the opposite page shows the perfect form Antoinette displayed as the world's greatest woman aerialist.

By the late twenties most circuses had abolished the regular street parade, but not the Ringling-owned Hagenbeck Wallace show which, in 1934, staged a long and beautiful parade the entire season.

This photograph, taken on May 17, 1934, shows the Hagenbeck Wallace parade in Peoria, Illinois.

From the 1940 season through the 1951 season not one circus gave a street parade as a daily feature.

This group picture of the entire personnel of the Greatest Show On Earth gives an idea of its vast size. That season (1934) the show toured the West Coast for the first time in five years.

RINGLING BROTHERS AND BARNUM & BAILEY COMBINED CIRCUS.

The West Coast was so hungry for a sight of the Big One that, despite the depression, crowds jammed the tent at every performance. Not for another five years did the show go that far west again.

Gargantua, the most publicized animal since Barnum's Jumbo, was a vicious, giant gorilla of incalculable strength. No one dared approach him, not even his trainer, Dick Kroener, who fed him daily for years and was once almost killed by him.

Gargantua's evil, twisted expression was caused by some acid thrown in his face when he was a baby. A pageant featuring Frank (Bring 'Em Back Alive) Buck was created in his honor when the 600-pound monster made his first appearance in 1938.

The career of Tom Mix (above, as a star on the Sells Floto show in 1930) reads like a western novel. According to his biographers Mix served in the Spanish-American War, became a Texas Ranger, western sheriff, U. S. Marshal, cowboy champion, and later a movie star and circus owner.

In 1934 he organized the Tom Mix Circus, a truck show with a cast of 150, starring himself and his horse, Tony Jr. The show made a record in 1936 by becoming the first to travel from coast to coast by motor. In 1938, the Black Year of circus history, the show closed and never returned to the road.

OFFICIAL ROUTE

Tim McCoy's REAL WILD WEST
AND ROUGH RIDERS OF THE WORLD

SEASON 1938 No. 1

Permanent Address
39 SO. LA SALLE STREET, CHICAGO, ILLINOIS

DATE	TOWN	STATE	R. R.	MILES
April 14	Chicago	Ill.	International Amphitheatre 43rd & Halsted	
" 15	"	"	" " " "	"
" 16	"	"	" " " "	"
" 17	"	"	" " " "	"
" 18	"	"	" " " "	"
" 19	"	"	" " " "	"
" 20	"	"	" " " "	"
" 21	"	"	" " " "	"
" 22	"	"	" " " "	"
" 23	"	"	" " " "	"
April 25	Columbus	Ohio	Penn R. R.	315
" 26	Dayton	"	"	70
" 27	Cincinnati	"	B. & O. R. R.	55
" 28	"	"	" " "	
" 29	Parkersburg	W. Va.	" " "	190
" 30	Clarksburg	"	" " "	81
May 2	Washington	D.C.	" " "	258
" 3	"	"	" " "	
" 4	"	"	" " "	
" 5	Baltimore	Md.	" " "	37
" 6	"	"	" " "	
" 7	Wilmington	Del.	Penn. R. R.	69
" 9	Philadelphia	Pa.	" " "	32
" 10	"	"	" " "	
" 11	"	"	" " "	
" 12	"	"	" " "	
" 13	"	"	" " "	
" 14	"	"	" " "	
			Total Miles to date 1,107	

That was the year that Tim McCoy, who had been featured on the Big One the previous two seasons, organized the last Wild West show to tour by rail. The 40-car outfit was the finest new show ever to take the road. McCoy spent $100,000 of his own money putting it together.

The above Number 1 route sheet was the only one issued by the ill-fated show. After a disastrous start in Chicago it limped to Washington and folded there on May 4. Eight shows closed early that season, one of which was the Big One. Only one big show (Al G. Barnes, Sells Floto) went all the way.

This photograph was taken on June 22, 1938, the day the Big One folded at Scranton, Pennsylvania.

Symbolic of the strike-crippled circus are the railroad tracks, signifying "the end of the line."

After the Big Show closed many performers joined the Ringling-owned Barnes-Sells Floto show in July.

A popular star at that time was Dorothy Herbert who jumped over flaming hurdles on a reinless horse.

226

Between 1926 and 1938 the Big Show had no wild animal acts except for the part-time appearances of Clyde Beatty. When they were revived as all-season, three-ring features the foremost trainer was the great Frenchman, Alfred Court (below, with a snow leopard casually draped around his neck).

A slight, suave man of infinite patience, Court never used a gun or chair, never raised his voice even when mixing species which were natural foes of each other (lions, tigers, leopards and Great Danes). A "trainer's trainer," Court is one of the very few who has never been badly hurt.

The tent burned for eight or nine minutes, then the six towering main poles and flaming canvas fell upon the trapped people inside.

These photographs (opposite page, and right) show the burning tent and fear-stricken people outside. Many who escaped fought to get back in, remembering people they had left inside.

There were many acts of heroism by performers and workmen but the disaster—the worst in circus history—took a terrible toll: 168 persons, two-thirds of them children, were either burned or trampled to death, and 487 were injured.

Criminal charges were inevitable. Six circus officials were tried and given prison sentences and the circus was fined $10,000. Damages awarded amounted to nearly $4,000,000, all of which was eventually paid. Below: The smouldering ruins.

On the afternoon of July 6, 1944, the Big One was playing in Hartford, Connecticut, before an audience of about 6,000, most of which were women and children. The show was only twenty minutes old when the Wallendas began their high wire act. Beneath them May Kovar, having finished her performance with Court's lions, was driving the cats through the steel-barred chute to their cages.

Suddenly a small flame was seen climbing up the canvas top. Someone yelled "Fire!" Merle Evans immediately switched to the tent-clearing number, *The Stars and Stripes Forever*. In another moment the fire was spreading across the whole paraffinned canvas surface with the roar of a forest fire. The crowd, now panic-stricken, rushed from the seats and broke into a stampede toward the exits.

After the Hartford fire the Big One returned to Sarasota, pulled itself together and in August returned to the road minus the big top. The show opened in the Rubber Bowl at Akron, Ohio, and for the rest of the season played in stadiums, baseball parks and fairgrounds, making stands of from two to four days in most cities. The shortened season ended at New Orleans in October.

The following spring the show started off with a bang by staging an old-time parade in New York (above), the first one the city had seen in twenty-five years. Many of the old wagons were put back in shape (including three band wagons) and the impressive parade, put on for the benefit of the Seventh War Loan, was a huge success. On the road the show played under a new flameproof canvas tent.

John Ringling North (above) became president of the Big Show in 1947 following a series of court battles for control of the circus that began shortly after the death of his uncle, John Ringling, in 1936. The office was not new to North. He had previously served as president for five years (1938-42). He was dropped in favor of his cousin, Robert Ringling, who represented an opposing faction of the three sets of fighting Ringling heirs, but was finally returned to the office which he now holds. His younger brother, Henry, is vice-president. The Norths are sons of the only Ringling girl, Ida, who married a railroad man named Henry W. North. She survived her seven brothers and was instrumental in gaining control of the show for her sons.

John North grew up in Baraboo, attended Yale for two years (class of '26), sold Florida real estate, tried Wall Street for awhile and then returned to Florida to help handle the tangled business affairs of his Uncle John. (The overextended Ringling could not meet interest payments on his loans and after the Florida and Wall Street crashes lost control of his circus.) When Ringling died, leaving a confused will that led to much litigation, North was named executor of the estate. He refinanced the circus and brought it back into the Ringling fold after five years of outside management.

Installed as president, North's influence was soon felt. The circus lost much of its traditional form, became more like a Broadway musicale.

Under the second North regime Art Concello, the flyer, became general manager. The diminutive aerialist (five feet, two inches) perfected a seating system which had been introduced years before by "Cap" Curtis for the Hagenbeck-Wallace show. Concello's improved mechanized seat wagon (left, with sides down and the built-in, metal seats collapsed) did away with the time-consuming task of erecting the wooden grandstand and the handling of thousands of chairs.

The photo below shows the wagon with sides extended and supported by posts, holding 300 people with an elephant in the aisle to demonstrate the strength of the unit. On the stairs (from left to right): John Ringling North, Art Concello and "Cap" Curtis who was then Ringling's boss canvasman.

Above: Rear view of a section of the twenty-nine wagons the show used when it played under canvas.

The interior of the wagons and the space between them were used for dressing rooms, as shown below.

As president John North would customarily go abroad every summer, confer with his European agent, Umberto Bedini, at the Ringling office in Paris and then make a Cadillac tour of the continent in search of acts. During the tour he would see some fifty circuses, innumerable variety shows and reviews, and would select about twenty acts. As a judge of talent North rates high. Among the many winners he has brought back are Francis Brunn (above), a juggler of astonishing skill, and (left) the great Austrian equilibrist, Unus, who in the center ring alone, does a hand stand on his forefinger (or perhaps on a steel brace concealed in his glove).

When Ringling played under canvas the most important tent to circus personnel was the cookhouse, a great mobile restaurant that served over 4,000 meals daily to some 1,400 people. The first tent to be taken down, it was packed at 5:30 p.m. and put aboard the Flying Squadron (first section of the train) along with the menagerie and working crews needed to set up the show at the next stand.

In contrast to the old field kitchen of the '90's (right), the Ringling cookhouse used the most modern equipment and was highly mechanized.

Barnum once stated that elephants and clowns are the pegs upon which circuses are hung. No circus could last a season without the funmakers, many of whom are talented artists, yet they are as a group the poorest paid performers, the hardest working (clowns appear eight or more times at every performance and make frequent costume changes), and they stand near the bottom in the circus caste system.

In the lingo of the big top the clown is a "Joey," a name given in honor of the famous English buffoon, Joseph Grimaldi (1778-1837).

No two clowns look exactly alike. Once a Joey originates a facial decoration he has a moral copyright on it and guards it jealously. The same is true of his costume.

Left: Felix Adler, "King of Clowns," in his basket costume. A producing clown (one who originates gags and props), Adler is more noted for his mirth-provoking antics with his pet pig.

The above elaborate gag costumes show "Mingo" as William Tell, and the dog-faced Buzzie Potts.

Below: The whiteface clowns, Lou Jacobs (originator of the midget auto act) and Paul Jerome.

A rarity in the Joey set was Rose Hanlon (above), a female clown. Facing her is the celebrated Albert White who designs and makes his own costumes.

Otto Griebling (with balloon) is, like Emmett Kelley and Fred Freeman, a blackface, or tramp comic. Below: Frankie Saluto, a Ringling midget.

Grotesque and ribald are the Hawaiian get-ups of these Sells Floto zanies.

Of the thirty-odd circuses currently operating in the United States (the number fluctuates from year to year) a half a dozen or so are "promotional" shows, i.e., they appear throughout the season under the sponsorship of some civic group or charity such as the Junior Chamber of Commerce, the American Legion and the Shrine, a Masonic order.

The most active and widespread sponsor is the Shrine which presents the various shows it engages as a "Shrine Circus," although the actual title may be Polack Brothers, Tom Packs, Orrin Davenport, Hamid-Morton or Clyde Brothers. (Most ticket holders are unaware of the show's proper name. To them it is simply the annual Shrine Circus.)

In general the arrangement between the Shrine and the circus works out like this: Shriners undertake advance ticket sales and pay certain costs. The show supplies the performance plus advance promotion. Predetermined costs of the circus are deducted from the gross. The remainder is divided between the circus and sponsor on a sliding-scale plan by which the Shrine might receive as much as seventy-five per cent of the profits.

Typical of a Shrine circus is Polack Brothers, a vest-pocket edition of the Big One. For over twenty years the show, which is split into Eastern and Western divisions, has been playing the year around under local auspices. Styled to play indoors or outdoors, it performs in armories, theaters, auditoriums, college stadiums, baseball parks and fair grounds. The fast-moving, well-organized show has offered such Ringling stars as the Wallendas, Unus, Alzana, the Justino Loyal Troupe, and many others.

Among its talented acts (left to right): The Goetche Brothers, the Namedils, the Sheridans.

The Shrine-sponsored Tom Packs Circus, like Polack Brothers, operates Eastern and Western units.

The above photograph of Packs' Alberto Zoppe Equestrian Troupe was taken in Toledo, in 1955.

Two inches of snow greeted the Mills Brothers opening at Greenville, Ohio, on April 18, 1953.

Below: Contortionist "Slim" Biggerstaff, and Al G. Kelly & Miller Brothers performer, Chief Keys.

These photographs of the tiny, Florida-based Benson Brothers Circus were taken in 1956, Fonda, New York, where the show was sponsored by the village fire department. The one-truck menagerie (below) offered (for twenty-five cents a head) one baby kangaroo, one small alligator and one large bunny.

America's oldest show operating under the same management is the spic and span Hunt Brothers Circus which was founded in 1892 by Charles T. Hunt (right) who has not missed a single performance since the show began. Year after year the three-ring affair, with a combined side show and menagerie, has played one-day stands from April to October in an area between Richmond, Virginia, and Boston. Working "under auspices" every season, the neat, wholesome show is welcomed back to the same towns yearly. Ever since it began as a horse and wagon show it has never permitted any grift or shortchanging to support its existence. One of the first shows to motorize, it now moves in thirty trucks, has a total personnel of 140, including a six-man band, and gives a two-and-a-half hour performance under its 100 by 225-foot, flameproof big top.

There have been many innovations by the Hunts, among them a helicopter used for advertising purposes. A consistent money-maker, the family-owned show is the last word in efficiency and dependability.

This photograph of the Hunt Brothers Grand Entry was taken nearly twenty-five years ago.

...cture of the same scene today would show little change except for noticeable improvement in equipment.

In contrast to the Hunt Brothers Grand Entry

is Ringling number, staged before a capacity crowd.

Sarasota, The Circus City

On Florida's West Coast about half way down the peninsula lies Sarasota, the Circus City, so named in 1927 when John and Charles Ringling moved the Big Show from Bridgeport, Connecticut, to its tropical home. Sarasota, which has a permanent population of some 33,000 and nearly three times that number during the winter months, is truly a Circus City. A tourist making the rounds of the unique city can see in one afternoon more circus than the average fan sees in a year.

He could visit the winter quarters of two circuses (Ringling and Cristiani Brothers), the state-operated Museum of the American Circus, in which is housed a valuable collection of circusiana, and the Circus Hall of Fame, a privately-owned commercial enterprise. Around town he would see numerous homes of circus people with performers practicing on back yard rigging, and three trailer camps inhabited entirely by circus folk, many of whom would be polishing their acts in public.

The 200-acre Ringling winter quarters is a year-around attraction, offering for 90 cents (children 50 cents) a Sunday afternoon two-hour show, a large menagerie, a museum of floats and a behind-the-scenes look at the circus. The weekly performance is staged in an open-air arena (called "Little Madison Square Garden" by show people). Here new acts are tried out—performing elephants, horses, dogs, the big cats, clown routines, bareback riders, acrobats and jugglers—and old acts are polished up.

Many of the Sunday performers are not with the Big One. They have been, perhaps, in the past but are now with other circuses, carnivals or night clubs and fill in with Ringling during the off-season.

Trevor Bale, shown above with his eleven tigers at winter quarters, has probably worked more species of animals than any living trainer. The list includes all of the big cats, elephants, giraffes, bears, llamas, zebras, the apes, horses, camels, dogs, and even an educated hippopotamus.

The Danish-born Bale, who was brought here by Ringling in 1953, began his circus life as a three-year old trick bicycle rider and has been performing constantly for forty years in more roles than he can recall. He has been a flyer, tight wire artist, juggler, equilibrist, clown and just about everything on the circus program. Bale, who has been bitten and mauled many times, says that tigers are the most dangerous cats to work. They spin faster and strike with less warning than any of the other cats, he says.

Right: Bale holds aloft his daughter, Bonny, the youngest of his four children.

The above photograph shows a herd of baby elephants stampeding on the Ringling track as handlers try to bring them under control. A moment before this picture was snapped the arena was filled with performers. All took cover when the stampede began.

Brought back in line (below, left), the still excited elephants are belabored by handlers. (The black-shirted man was knocked down, has just regained his feet.) One handler, squeezed between two elephants, suffered crushed ribs (below).

Although elephants have tender skins and are sensitive to the slightest touch they willingly submit to a blowtorch singeing. (The long hairs are singed off to make the hide smooth for an oil rubdown which preserves the skin and prevents shedding.)

All circus elephants are called "bulls," regardless of sex and almost without exception come from India. The African elephants are larger, have enormous fan-like ears and are difficult to handle. The few Africans with American circuses are used only for display purposes.

The more docile Indian elephant is a good performer, learns tricks quickly and well and remembers them years after he has given them up. In intelligence he ranks high among the mammals and is topped only by the chimpanzee and the orangutan. The legend that an elephant never forgets past injuries has little foundation, however.

His life span is about the same as our own, although some bulls have reached 130 years in captivity. The average bull is from eight to ten feet high at the shoulders and eats 125 pounds of hay daily.

Many old Ringling performers, having spent years on the road, come back to the Circus City and make their homes there. Among them is Captain William Heyer (above, with his 16-hand dancing horse, Royal Rex Shine) who now operates a riding academy on land adjacent to the Ringling winter quarters. A former Dutch cavalry officer, Heyer was for many years an outstanding high-school rider on the Big One. (High-school riding is so named because the various steps the horse performs are usually taught in academies.) Heyer was noted for his faultless seat and hands, and his ability to put his mount through the most complicated steps with a minimum of pressure from reins, knees and spurs.

A more recent master of the dancing horse is Alexander Konyot (left), who, like his father before him, rated the Ringling center ring.

On the opposite page is Czeslan Mroczkowski (Charlie Moroski to circusdom), a renowned liberty horse trainer. (A liberty act consists of a number of riderless horses that respond to a verbal command or the crack of a whip.) Moroski uses stallions which were bred at the King Ranch in Texas.

Spectators at Ringling's Little Madison Square Garden see some odd sights when the Big Show is in rehearsal—such as the scene above of these newly arrived chorus girls who have obviously not yet learned to keep in step.

The directing, staging and choreographing of the annual production is done by Richard Barstow (below) and his sister, Edith. The Barstows spend about four months planning each new show, then come to Sarasota for a few weeks of intensive work.

High above the rehearsing chorines Pinito Del Oro
tunes up her act on the swaying trapeze.

Pinito, who works without a net, was "discovered"
by John North in a small Spanish roadside show.

Strolling about the park-like grounds of the vast Ringling winter quarters, visitors often come upon a zany scene like the one depicted on the opposite page, of Lou Jacobs sharing his newspaper with a kibitzing giraffe.

In the nearby indoor riding ring the Mexican dwarf, Cha-cha, approaches his horse and then with the "mechanic" attached to his waist—a safety device to prevent a bad fall—puts on a comic riding act.

In the indoor riding ring the Justino Loyal Troupe starts practicing for the coming season by forming a relatively simple pyramid of four persons and two horses. (Note the mechanic worn by top-mounter Justino Loyal. The device is not used on the road.)

The act reaches fulfillment (opposite page) with five horses and a three-high galloping pyramid of eight persons. Justino Loyal stands in the center of the pyramid, supporting the topmost rider. He first appeared in this country in 1946.

The spade-bearded Mennonites who appear to be looking across the page at Beatrice Dante and her trained chimpanzee are members of a colony of the Plain People who dwell in the Circus City. Many of the sect are circus fans and they can be seen daily at winter quarters strolling about the grounds in their strange, somber garments.

The first Mennonite family came to Sarasota in the winter of 1925. They returned the following year bringing a few friends with them to work the celery farms, and over the years the number gradually increased. Now there are more than 100 families of the Plain People living in the Circus City the year around.

The daring young men on the flying trapeze are among the first to show up at winter quarters to begin the daily two-hour grind of polishing up their old stunts and trying out new ones.

The smiling Juan Rodriguez (above), a veteran flyer, has just executed a perfect fall—purposely made at his first tune-up session.

The first thing a novice flyer must learn is to fall properly, for a head foremost plunge into the net almost always results in a broken neck, and a skidding belly-whopper causes severe rope burns and torn muscles. Landing feet foremost can mean broken ankles. A flyer tries to land on his back to prevent injury. Failing this, he rolls himself up into a ball and trusts to luck.

The Sabrejets, a three-man flying act (left), loosen up before going aloft. Left to right: Catcher Dick Anderson, Billy Ward and Rodriguez .

Rodriguez (above, in net), somewhat rusty after a two-month layoff, has just taken another plunge—this time it was unplanned—and discusses the cause of the mishap with Anderson and members of Clayton Behee's Falcons, another flying troupe.

The all-important net is nine feet from the ground, covers the area beneath the rigging's uprights and carries upwards beyond that space, thus giving further protection should a flyer lose his grip in a long swing and get shot beyond.

Rodriguez and Anderson apply rosin to their hands before trying their "cutaway" to a stick stunt (shown below). Here Rodriguez wears a mechanic about his waist, from which the two side ropes run through pulleys to the hands of a man standing alongside the net. It is his job to apply leverage to the ropes if the flyer misses—as Rodriguez has in this scene—and to slow up his fall into the net. Primarily used for safety, the mechanic gives a performer more confidence to attempt new tricks. He knows that he cannot seriously injure himself in a fall.

In the spectacular "passing leap" one leaper flies over the other as they trade catcher for trapeze.

Here Rodriguez (right) completes leap from catcher to trapeze which Ward (center) has just left.

Gone from the winter quarters scene ever since Ringling gave up playing under canvas is the huge tent factory, or "sail loft," which formerly employed a crew of skilled craftsmen the year around.

Here the big top and the more than thirty other tents that comprised the canvas city were made. Each year a new big top emerged from the tent factory. The last one, designed by Leif Osmundson for the 1956 season, was 406 feet long, 206 feet wide and consisted of fourteen pieces, each of which weighed just under a ton for a total weight of about 28,000 pounds dry and at least double that when wet.

Two big tops from previous years were always kept on hand when the new one was shipped north in May. One was used for rehearsals at winter quarters, the other was stored ready to be sent out to replace the traveling tent, or sections of it, should an emergency arise on the road.

Today the half empty sail loft is a workshop where blankets for horses and elephants are made.

When the Big One moved on rails scores of train-men, painters, carpenters, mechanics and electricians were kept busy repairing equipment for the annual tour. (Below: Workers repair aerialists' net.)

Every year the show's seventy-odd double-length railroad cars, which moved in three sections, were painted (above) and thoroughly overhauled. (Below: A cat pushes a circus wagon into the machine shop.)

Clown Harry Rusta shows how to get into high stilts. Having mounted seat wagon, he descends into stilts (1), takes costume (2), puts it on (3), fastens it (4), strolls over to chat with friend (5).

The above photograph, taken in the big top at winter quarters in March, 1956, shows aerial director Barbette instructing a Japanese girl in a ballet number. (This was the last year a full-size big top was set up on the Ringling lot. Performers now practice in the former car barn and other buildings but the Sunday shows and dress rehearsals are staged in the outdoor arena as before.)

Barbette, whose square name is Vanderclyde Broadway, was born in Texas, became a female impersonator and in girl's costume and wig won acclaim in Europe as a single trapeze and tight wire artist. He also did an iron jaw act. Since his retirement he has been employed as aerial director for Ringling and other shows.

Bruises and sprains are common during the early stages of the aerial ballet rehearsals. The two casualties shown on the right are Kim Eggenschwiler (on crutches) and Carole June Bilter.

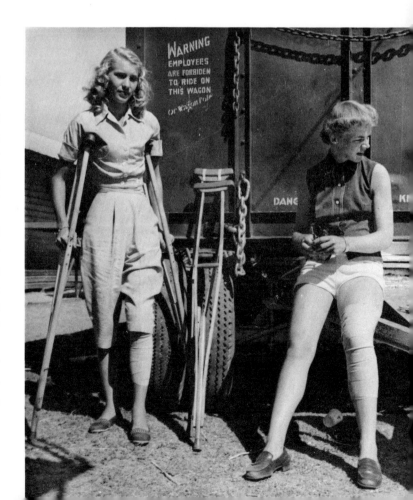

A circus must have showgirls as well as clowns and elephants. Pirkko Ussim, Finnish platinum-haired beauty, doubled as showgirl and assistant to her Danish husband, Hans, in a liberty horse act.

Unhappy midget clown Harry Burman puts on elephant's hind legs (1), takes position behind leader, Sonny Reilly (2) and completes costume (3) for walkaround rehearsal on outdoor arena (4).

One of the all-professional trailer camps in the Circus City is owned by Joe Maschino, a retired acrobat (above). English is rarely spoken at Maschino's 23-acre camp where performers from Europe and the Orient make their homes in the off-season and practice their acts for circuses and carnivals.

In an average season about fifty performers representing a dozen nationalities live in the camp's twenty-five trailers. Maschino charges $20 a month for parking a trailer, $60 a month to rent one.

Below: The Four Whirlwinds, tumbling act from Germany, practice alongside their trailer.

The Del-Rae's practice their rotating perch act.   When performing they are ninety feet aloft.

Unassisted by any balancing apparatus and with no net beneath him, Takeo Usui walks barefooted on a cable strung from the top of a pine tree to the door of his trailer at Maschino's. The Japanese daredevil first appeared on the Big Show in 1955.

When Usui loses his balance he does a handstand (opposite page), then resumes the climb. In his act he wears slippers and leather tights, walks twice to the very top of the arena and slides down—the first time sitting, the second time standing.

Pancho, the only motorcycle-riding dog in the world, takes a spin but is ignored by performers.

Trainer Oglie Zavatta (below) lives in a bus at Maschino's with his family and fourteen dogs.

Down the road a piece from Maschino's camp and less than a mile from the Ringling lot are the winter quarters of the Cristiani Brothers Circus, a family-owned show that roams from Key West, Florida, to Canada's maritime provinces and finishes the season in the Circus City in late October.

The Cristianis are not only the most talented circus family, they are the largest and oldest, boasting five generations of performers. Wizards of bareback riding, tumbling, juggling, the high trapeze and perch, the Cristianis are the Royal Family of Circusdom. They own seven homes in Sarasota. The expanding family now numbers more than fifty actual performers, too many to appear with any single circus. Cristiani units are spread across the country, playing night clubs, theaters, movies and circuses.

The poster on the opposite page depicts the Italian-born Cristianis when they first appeared in this country in 1934. (John Ringling had spotted them when they were playing in Belgium the previous year.)

Lucio Cristiani (right), great grandson of the first performing Cristiani, manages the circus, doubles as a bareback rider. Counting in-laws, brothers and sisters, he has fifteen relatives in the show.

Lucio Cristiani is the only man who has ever perfected a full twist somersault from one horse to another. It is no ordinary somersault in which the body is doubled up and does not change its axis. In the full twist Lucio's body is almost straight and while somersaulting in that position he simultaneously twists once around, or pirouettes, before landing. Difficult under any circumstances, it was thought impossible to do from horse to horse.

The Cristianis have done the impossible many times, notably in their "suicide" act which took three years to develop. In this breath-taker three Cristianis, each on a galloping horse one behind the other, throw somersaults through hoops at the same instant and land one place behind, the performer on the rear horse alighting on the ground. At the finish of the stunt the lead horse has no rider, the second and third are occupied.

Ronnie Henon (above, practicing his act at winter quarters and performing on the road) was a high school boy living in John Day, Oregon, when the Bailey and Cristiani Circus came to town in 1954. An amateur juggler, Ronnie got permission from the Cristianis to do his act at the circus performance before his home town friends. It went over well and two weeks later when school let out Ronnie joined up. That season the show made what is probably the longest overland jump in circus history—from Casper, Wyoming, to Anchorage, Alaska, a distance of 2,850 miles. Ronnie went along. He took a year out to finish high school, then rejoined the show and he has been with it ever since, clowning and juggling.

Bagonghi (right), a dwarf clown who has been with the Cristiani family since 1920, claims that he has played in all countries of Europe and North America. Like many a trouper he carries all his belongings in one trunk. On the dwarf's tiny trunk in large red letters is written:

THE GREAT BAGONGHI.

The photographs on these two pages, taken at winter quarters, depict some of the many roles played by Barbara Fairchild, Cristiani Brothers' all-around circus girl.

The daughter of a well-to-do Canadian rancher, Barbara was born in Calgary in 1933 and began riding her father's horses before she was of school age. The family moved to Galt, Ontario, where Barbara grew up and appeared in local fairs and shows on high-school horses, and as a trick rider.

Circus-struck, she left home at nineteen and entrained for Sarasota alone, hoping to get a job on the Big One in a bareback act. There was no opening for her that season (1952) so Barbara went to Macon, Georgia, then the winter quarters of the King Brothers and Cristiani Circus. (The show had advertised in *Billboard*, the leading weekly of the amusement world, for a trick rider.) She got the job but little realized the multiple duties she was expected to fulfill as a circus trouper.

Barbara began her career as the leader of the King-Cristiani daily parade (1952-3), has worked trained animals (bears, elephants, ponies), performed in the aerial ballet and as a bareback, high-school and trick rider, designed and made costumes and has acted as ticket seller and candy butcher.

In the sequence of pictures on this page the Cristianis are shown practicing their teeter board act.

Turning a back somersault to a three-high stand, Ortans is catapulted to her brother's shoulders.

The five Cristiani brothers and sister Ortans do their famous four-high stand at a rainy afternoon performance at Herkimer, New York, on July 23, 1956, four months after the practice session at winter quarters (opposite page).

Here, Paul, having just leaped from the table off Belmonte's shoulders, hits the board, on the other end of which Ortans was standing. (Table is steadied by circus worker, far right.) As Ortans takes off Paul and Belmonte rush forward to catch her should the pyramid collapse.

Hurled eighteen feet high, Ortans is about to light on Lucio's shoulders. As he reaches out to seize her by the legs, Daviso, the understander, looks up at his revolving sister. Between Lucio and Daviso stands Oscar, ready for the impact.

Ortans is the only woman who ever did a triple somersault from teeter board to four-high. She used to do the stunt regularly but has recently given it up and now does only the single.

The Cristianis leave the Circus City in mid-March but the Big Show remains a couple of weeks longer before packing up for New York.

In the last minute rush to get off the busiest man on the Ringling lot is J.Y. "Doc" Henderson, shown above inoculating one of the 200 horses in his charge. Since his duties began he has treated almost every species of animal that can live in captivity and has acted as general practitioner, dentist, surgeon and midwife. He has performed amputations (among them an alligator's leg), set fractured limbs and tails and has pulled teeth from lions, tigers and chimpanzees. The elephants are his most cooperative patients. Most difficult: Zebras. Left: Doc coaxes a burro to board railroad car.

The circus cars were all loaded and ready to roll out of winter quarters at 1 p.m. on March 29, 1956, when animal keepers sounded the alarm that Ingrid, the lady giraffe, was about to add another member to the menagerie. Doc Henderson rushed to the flat car on which Ingrid's wagon was lashed and had the cage removed and hauled by bulldozer to the giraffe winter barn (right). A half an hour later Ingrid gave birth to a wobbly-legged son. (The above photograph was taken a few minutes after his birth.)

The event disrupted the precision loading and departure of the train, caused a two-hour delay. Ingrid and her son joined the circus weeks later.

The day before the Big One moves out of the Circus City the cats and bears are transferred from their winter cages to wagons which are then loaded on to flat cars and lashed tight to prevent any movement while the train is under way. Extra precaution is taken when the bears are transferred, for keepers know that they are the most unpredictable and most deadly of all the wild animals.

Unlike the cat who, as a rule, launches a single spurt attack and then quits or is subdued, the bear will fight ceaselessly until his victim is destroyed. Nothing can make him loose his hold once he has his teeth set in a man—not even a stream of water or a blank cartridge fired in his face. The lumbering, seemingly good natured bear is at heart a killer, the most vicious animal in the circus menagerie.

Left: Workers fix a flat tire on one of the loaded circus wagons. Since 1934 the Ringling wagons have rolled on rubber tires.

Horses and elephants are loaded aboard the circus train on the day of departure as usual. This procedure has not changed since Ringling gave up the big top. The menagerie continues to go north with the show for the New York and Boston stands but it returns to Sarasota after that and remains there the rest of the year.

Sprinkling holy water on the Ringling train, the Reverend Martin Powell, assistant pastor of St. Martha's Parish, performs the traditional custom of blessing the circus on the day of departure. (Similar rites are performed on the Cristiani lot when the show's trucks roll out to start the season.)

The photographs on these two pages were taken in 1956, the last year the entire circus personnel moved by rail. The first train section, consisting of eighteen cars for about 400 performers, eight livestock cars for the menagerie and sixteen flats loaded with equipment, left Sarasota on March 29. The second section of thirty-eight cars carrying the big top, cook tent and other outdoor equipment left on May 16 and joined the show in Baltimore for the first outdoor performance on May 20.

Delayed by the birth of the giraffe, performers had extra time to chat with their friends who came out to winter quarters to see them off (above). Meanwhile crowds waited for the train in Sarasota.

On the Sarasota-New York run the Doll Family plays poker in an upper berth while the tatooed man,

Ramus Neilson, chats with Betty Broadbent and Alice from Dallas devours cookies in her bunk.

Jammed in three-tier bunks (about 80 men to a car), the roustabouts did not travel in style.

These photographs, taken a few seasons ago, record scenes that will never again take place.

7 On The Road

The Cristianis, first of the tented circuses to go on the road (in March), are followed by a score of other shows, among the last being the Hunt Brothers Circus which does not customarily open until late April.

With a brand-new big top measuring 245 by 115 feet and a menagerie-side-show tent (above), the Cristianis began the 1956 season at West Palm Beach, on March 12 and covered 14,110 miles in thirty trucks before closing in Sarasota on October 21 to complete a highly successful tour. The same general route (Florida to Canada) was repeated in 1957.

Left: Cristiani performers Fred Cannestrelli and Tommy Parris (doing flip) warm up before going on.

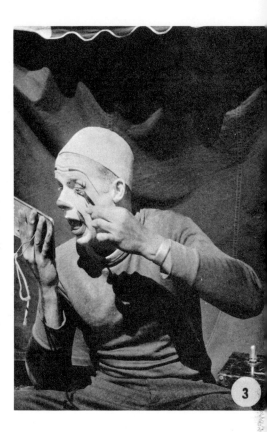

Sandy-haired Harry Dann, former Ringling clown, applies makeup for Cristiani's Grand Entry.

Dann doffed his clown costume in midseason, 1956, for the role of equestrian director and announcer.

These "back yard" scenes of the Cristiani circus on the road show (above) Marion Cristiani, Oscar's wife, who works one of the best elephant acts in the country and doubles as the show's wardrobe mistress, and (below) car-loading of kids who will get free seats for taking part in jammed auto act.

Animal keeper Earl "Irish" Greer survived an attack by an elephant but was left permanently crippled. The elephant did a headstand on him, broke both legs and several ribs.

Formerly a Mexican school teacher, Carlos Leal, the fire-eater, literally warms up for his act.

While the Cristianis were heading north in the spring of 1956 with a good season assured, Clyde Beatty (right) was having trouble with his 15-car railroad show out in California. A disastrous Los Angeles stand followed by a series of mishaps, bad weather, poor houses and a strike caused him to throw in the sponge at Burbank on May 9 after forty-three days on the road.

Meanwhile in the East the King Brothers Circus labored along with two units (Eastern and Western) though burdened by debts incurred the previous year when it lost $125,000, and a government tax claim of about $100,000 against it. The show never had a chance. First to fold was the Western unit (in May), and the Eastern succumbed a few weeks later, leaving equipment stranded in Connecticut (below).

Although the Clyde Beatty Circus had listed debts of $280,000 against assets of $260 at its bankruptcy petition, the show reorganized in August and had a successful tour before closing in November at its new winter quarters at De Land, Florida.

The Ringling circus got off to a good start in the early stages of the New York run despite picketing by the Teamsters Union and the American Guild of Variety Artists. But toward the end of the stand business fell off badly. The show moved on to Boston where the vindictive unions staged a competing circus in the city's 7,200-seat Arena, charging $1.50 a ticket (kids free) against Ringling's $4 tops.

Side Show talker Bobby Hassen (above, with Josephine Royal, Mexican snake charmer, on the platform) did more than introduce the acts after the show's first stand under canvas (Baltimore, May 22). Hassen was given the task of announcing to the waiting crowds that the scheduled 2:15 matinee performance would be delayed—which it was, from one to four hours at almost every stand.

Plagued by railroad difficulties and shortage of roustabouts, the slow-moving circus headed north along the eastern seaboard on eighty cars, playing to light houses at the curtailed matinees. More than a dozen performers had dropped out of the show rather than cross picket lines, among them clowns Emmett Kelly, Felix Adler and Otto Greibling. None of the key acts, however, quit the show.

Outstanding among those who stayed with it was the high wire artist, Harold Alzana (above) and (right), with Jimmy Armstrong, a midget clown who doubled as a bugler by blowing the warning calls before every show to alert the performers.

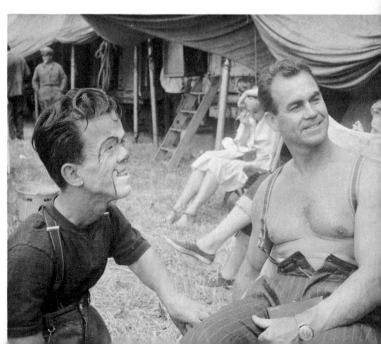

These back stage glimpses of the Big One during its last tour under canvas depict (above) aerialist Dick Anderson hanging up his white tights as Gena Moroski watches a chorus boy knit a sweater.

Below: Roustabouts line up for commissary tickets; Minnie Alzana takes a shampoo in a bucket.

Traveling west across New York State the show continued to get more than its share of misfortune. But back stage activity went on as usual, as evidenced by these pictures which show Hans Ussim walking a liberty horse and (right) a blacksmith shoeing a horse between performances at Utica, June 27.

Bad luck followed the show. At Geneva on July 1 a sudden wind ripped open the big top from end to end, injuring fifteen people. In several towns after that performances were given without a tent. There was a cancellation at Buffalo because of storm warnings, and at Meadville, Pennsylvania, two performances were given without seats.

'Greatest Show On Earth' Holds Final Performance In Big Top

Rumors that the show might close grew stronger when John Ringling North caught up with it aboard his private car at Alliance, Ohio, on July 15. Next day he dropped the bombshell. In an abrupt announcement to the press he put an end to the show, adding that "the tented circus is a thing of the past."

On the afternoon of July 16, on a drab parking lot at the Heidelberg Raceway on the outskirts of Pittsburgh, Ringling's great tented city was put up for the last time (above). Stunned performers gathered for the final matinee, knowing that next day the circus train would be heading for Sarasota.

That night a capacity audience of 10,000 saw the last performance under canvas (above). As the crowd made for the exits shortly after midnight the band struck up *Auld Lang Syne* and a few minutes later roustabouts began pulling down the tents.

It took three long days for the "funeral" train to get back home. Hundreds of Sarasotans met it at the station with welcoming signs, and a band played a march. But the gaiety was forced. In everyone's mind was the question, "Is this the end of the show?"

It was not the end of the show if John Ringling North was to be believed. At the Pittsburgh closing he had stated that the circus would open next season in Madison Square Garden as usual, but would thereafter play only in air conditioned arenas.

Circus people were more hopeful of the show's future when North appointed Art Concello (above) as Executive Director. An old pro (unlike his inexperienced predecessor, Michael Burke), Concello is one of the most capable circus men in the business.

Although circus fans lauded the appointment of Concello their criticism of North continued. Admitting that there were some things to his credit the charges against him were many: He had "Hollywoodized" the traditional circus, made it into a second-rate revue. He had dropped the vital outdoor advertising and had in general mismanaged the whole affair. Furthermore, they said, he had fired many qualified people who had been with the show for years and had replaced them with inexperienced outsiders.

One who has weathered North's purges is Pat Valdo (right, as a clown about 1910; below, as he looks today, with his assistant Bob Dover). Born Patrick Fitzgerald, Valdo first joined the Ringling show in 1904, worked as clown, juggler, wire walker, became assistant ringmaster and was made director of personnel in 1929.

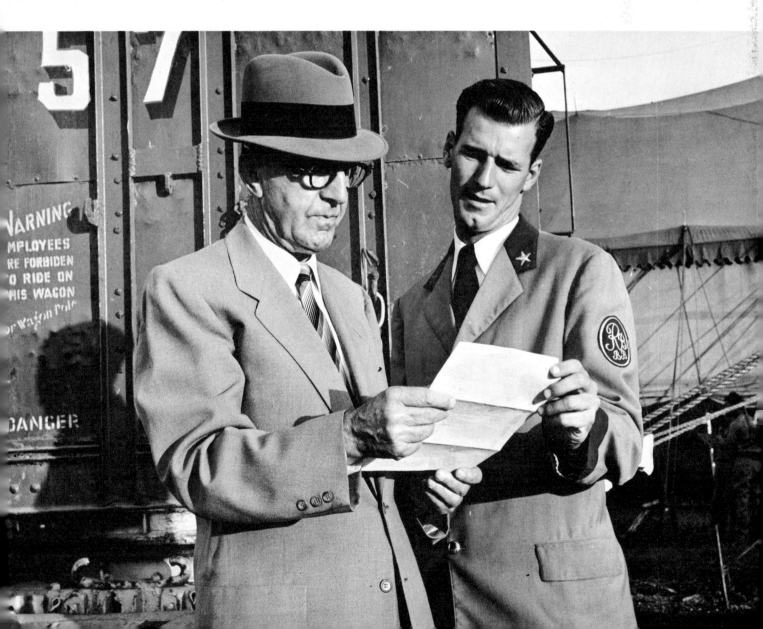

Tonito, forward somersaulting star, was among the   first to be engaged by Valdo for the 1957 edition.

Facing its most critical season in eighty-seven years, the Big Show went into rehearsal at winter quarters with a new look. A noticeable change—built around the fact that the circus would play mostly indoors—was the transformation of the old car barn into a miniature Madison Square Garden for practice sessions (below).

With less fanfare than any previous year the show moved out of Sarasota on March 28 on fifteen cars (three sleepers, eight flats, four stock cars) for the April 3 opening in New York. Left behind were some sixty railroad cars, replaced by Ringling's new fleet of trucks (right). No longer could the Big One be called a railroad show.

HIGHLIGHTS OF

Two events made news as the 1957 season got underway: In a reverse play clown Emmett Kelly (above) ran away from the circus and joined the Brooklyn Dodgers, and for the first time in eighty-six years the season began without a single railroad circus in operation.

It is unlikely that any circus will ever again move on rails. But circus fans were not dismayed.

To their joy the new Ringling show regained its old-time circus flavor with a production frankly aimed at children. Meanwhile the rejuvenated Beatty circus got off to a strong start, as did most of the other shows in the land. The railroad era may be over and the Big One may not seem quite the same without canvas, say circus fans, but as long as there are children there will always be a circus.

List of Circuses

COMPILED BY TOM PARKINSON

CIRCUS EDITOR, THE BILLBOARD

Uncounted hundreds of circuses have operated in America. Many disappeared almost as soon as they were conceived, but others brought fun to their patrons and fame for their owners. Among them were both large and small shows, those that were known throughout the nation and those that enjoyed applause of regional audiences. Certain of these shows stand out above the others in the complex meanderings of sale, collapse, combination and squeeze-out that have brought American circuses from the time of John Bill Ricketts to that of John Ringling North. They are listed here, the most significant shows in American circus history.

BUD E. ANDERSON SHOWS

As Indian Bud's Wild West, it began about 1922 and became a circus two years later. Trucks began replacing wagons in 1927. Known as Seal Bros. Circus by the 1930s, it made great profits in Western territory during the depression. Title in the 1940s was Bud E. Anderson's Jungle Oddities Circus. The owner was killed in a truck accident July 4, 1950, and his son continued the show two more years.

ATTERBURY BROS. CIRCUS

Operated for a generation by Robert L. Atterbury, closing about 1937 and subsequently operated briefly by his family. His sons and daughter became performers with leading shows thereafter.

GEORGE F. BAILEY CIRCUS

Final operation of the Flatfoot syndicate. Bailey was with the Aron Turner Circus and inherited that show in the 1850s. Operated under his own title for many years ending in 1875 and was linked with the Flatfoots late in that period. He directed the Flatfoot operation of the Barnum show prior to its sale to James A. Bailey who was no relation.

MOLLIE BAILEY CIRCUS

Confederate nurse and wife of composer of "The Old Grey Mare," Mollie began her circus shortly after the Civil War with a wagon show, changed to four railroad cars in 1907. Mollie owned property in about 150 Texas towns and used her own land as showgrounds in each town. Her sons took over management about 1915, changed to trucks for 1919 and closed shortly thereafter.

AL G. BARNES CIRCUS

An animal trainer, Barnes expanded his single act into a carnival show and, in 1910, into a ten-car circus, which toured the West. This show had the famous outlaw elephant, Tusko, and was famed for its wide variety of trained animal acts. Grew to 30-car size. Sold after 1928 season to the American Circus Corporation, which operated it in 1929 and then sold, along with its other holdings, to John Ringling. Operated as a Ringling subsidiary thru 1938. In its final years it went thru title gymnastics that had it called Al G. Barnes-Sells Floto in 1937 and 1938; Al G. Barnes-Sells Floto & John Robinson Combined Circuses in some cases during 1938, and finally (after a strike closed Ringling-Barnum), Al G. Barnes-Sells Floto Circus with Ringling Bros. and Barnum & Bailey Stupendous New Features—surely the most high-powered set of circus names ever on a single show.

BARNETT BROS. CIRCUS

Founded in Canada in 1927 and moved to the U.S. in 1929. Operated by Ray W. Rogers. Retitled Wallace Bros. Circus for 1937 and 1941-44. In 1943 it was combined with Clyde Beatty Circus. Rogers died that year and employees operated it in 1944, then sold the equipment to Beatty and King circuses.

BARNUM & BAILEY CIRCUS

Founded in 1871 by William C. Coup and associates as P. T. Barnum Circus. In 1872 it became the first circus to operate regularly as a railroad show using its own railroad cars. Operated by Barnum alone but disastrously in 1874, and thereafter leased to others through 1880. Combined with Cooper & Bailey Circus in 1881, and known as Barnum & London Circus through 1887. James A. Bailey became controlling partner in 1888, when show was renamed Barnum & Bailey Greatest Show on Earth. It had Jumbo 1882-1885. Bailey became sole owner. Toured Europe 1897-1902 and returned for battle with Ringling Bros. Circus for Eastern U.S. territory. Bailey died in 1906 and show was acquired by the Ringlings before the 1908 season. Operated as a separate show thru 1918, and combined to form Ringling Bros. and Barnum & Bailey Circus in 1919.

BATCHELOR & DORIS CIRCUS

John B. Doris and George F. Batchelor, who had operated concessions on other big shows, founded the Batchelor & Doris Circus in 1879. After 1882 it was the John B. Doris Inter-Ocean Circus, and it failed in 1888 as the Doris & Colvin Circus.

CLYDE BEATTY CIRCUS

Originated in 1943 as the motorized Clyde Beatty-Wallace Bros. Circus and 1944 Clyde Beatty-Russell Bros. Circus. It was a 15-car railroad show, entitled Clyde Beatty Circus, 1945 to 1956. Animal-trainer Beatty closed it in May, 1956; subsequently it was sold and reopened in the fall of 1956. Since this was after the close of Ringling-Barnum, it was the only railroad circus on tour that year. It switched to trucks for 1957, still under management of Frank McClosky and Walter Kernan and featured Beatty in his wild animal act.

BEERS-BARNES CIRCUS

Founded as a repertoire show in 1932 and later transformed into a circus. Operated to date by Mrs. George Beers, her son, Charles Beers, son-in-law, Roger Barnes, and families. Motorized.

BENSON BROS. CIRCUS

A current circus in the smaller class. Operated by William Morris. Formerly known as Kelly-Morris Circus.

BUCKLEY & WEEKS CIRCUS

One of the earliest tented circuses in the U.S., operating in the 1830s.

BUFFALO BILL WILD WEST SHOW

Founded in 1883 by William F. (Buffalo Bill) Cody and others. Nate Salsbury soon became a partner.

The unique show was widely copied by other showmen. It moved by rail from the start but often played long engagements, such as the one of many weeks in 1893, across from the main gate of the Chicago World's Fair. Toured England in 1887, and performed for Queen Victoria. Lacking mobility as well as a partner by 1895, Cody induced James A. Bailey to equip and route the show in exchange for half interest, and Bailey used much of the Forepaugh-Sells Circus equipment to operate the Cody show. In 1903 the Buffalo Bill Show began a four-year tour of Europe. Following Bailey's death, his share evolved to Pawnee Bill (Lillie) and the title became the Buffalo Bill Wild West and Pawnee Bill Great Far East Show, touring from 1907 into 1913, when it collapsed in mid-season. The title has been used spasmodically since in such instances as Sells Floto-Buffalo Bill Circus, Buffalo Bill & Miller Bros. 101 Ranch Wild West, Buffalo Bill Wild West & Circus with Jess Willard, and Hagenbeck-Wallace Circus & Buffalo Bill Wild West. The name also has been usurped frequently by showmen in Europe, Africa and South America.

CAMPBELL BROS. CIRCUS

Operated out of Fairbury, Nebraska, starting as a wagon show in 1893 and closing as a 20-car railroad circus in 1912.

CARSON & BARNES CIRCUS

A small circus touring the West. Operated by Jack Moore.

CHRISTY BROS. CIRCUS

Began in 1910 as a tented vaudeville-movie show and switched to circus in 1914 as Christy's Big Hippodrome Shows. In 1919, George W. Christy began adding to the original two-car show. In three years there were seven cars; by 1925 the show reached its peak of 20 cars. In mid-season 1930 half of the train was sent home, but the reduction was not enough to save the show from the depression, and it folded in July that season. Equipment was sold later to Cole Bros.

M. L. CLARK CIRCUS

Operated in the South as a wagon show from the 1890s until World War I. Title subsequently used by others on railroad and truck shows.

CLYDE BROS. CIRCUS

An indoor circus currently in operation and playing under local sponsors at arenas in the Middle West, Southwest and Ontario. Operated by Howard Suesz.

COLE BROS. CIRCUS

Title created by Martin Downs for his show of 1906-1908. Later Al G. Campbell, Elmer Jones, John Pluto, and Floyd King were among those using the title on various shows. In 1935, Jess Adkins and Zack Terrell built a new circus with equipment from Christy and Robbins shows and elsewhere and they called it Cole Bros. This big show continued thru 1948, when Terrell sold it to Jack Tavlin. After 1949 it was sold to Arthur M. Wirtz and associates. The show folded after its unsuccessful tour in 1950. The title has been used regularly in variation by other shows. King Bros. & Cole Bros. Circus was the billing for the King show in 1955. Famous Cole Circus, on trucks, toured in 1957. There have been dozens of other uses of the name Cole in circus titles.

FAMOUS COLE CIRCUS

A current circus playing Western and Middle Western states under management of Herb Walters. Founded in 1950 as the Cole & Walters Circus and later known as the George W. Cole Circus.

W. W. COLE CIRCUS

Founded in 1871 as Cole & Orton Circus. Became the first circus to play many Western towns when its train pressed on the heels of rail builders. Owner W. W. Cole auctioned his show in 1886 in order to accept a position with Barnum & Bailey. Some equipment went to form Lemen Bros. Circus. Cole, credited with being the first man to make a million dollars in circus business, inspired many other "Cole" titles used since.

COOP & LENT CIRCUS

Began in 1916 as a railroad circus. Under different management in 1917. Operated in 1918 as a pioneer motorized circus and failed because of inability to get delivery on more trucks after World War I began.

COOPER & BAILEY CIRCUS

A progression of circus deals and titles led to Cooper & Bailey Circus of 1874, with James A. Bailey and James E. Cooper as owners. Toured Australia in 1876-1877, then Netherlands East Indies and Java the next year. Followed with tour of South America in 1878. En route home it bought Howes' Great London Circus, and these were combined for the next two seasons. Then Bailey and Barnum combined their shows in 1881.

W. C. COUP SHOWS

After Coup and Barnum parted, Coup operated small shows in the 1880s and 1890s.

CRISTIANI BROS. CIRCUS

Cristiani Family of bareback riders appeared with several U.S. shows after 1934 and became partner in King Bros. Circus in 1948. Title was King Bros. & Cristiani for 1952-1953. The Cristianis started own show in 1954 as Bailey Bros. & Cristiani, playing ballparks rather than in a tent, and traveled by truck. It became the first circus to appear in Alaska, motoring up the Alcan Highway. In 1956 the title became Cristiani Bros. Circus and the show was reorganized as an under-canvas operation.

DAILEY BROS. CIRCUS

Became first show to switch from trucks to trains, altho many made the opposite change. Dailey Bros. was a railroad show from 1944 until mid-season of 1950, when it folded after a disasterous tour of Canada. Joe Louis, the heavyweight champion, was featured part of the final year. Show-owner B. C. Davenport toured motorized shows in subsequent years.

ORRIN DAVENPORT SHOWS

Started in 1906 when Orrin Davenport was a star bareback rider with Ringling Bros. Circus and he began producing indoor circuses in the winters for Shrine sponsors. He and his family continued their riding act until 1937. In the meantime his indoor route grew, and he now devotes full time to it. The Orrin Davenport Circus, appearing under a different local sponsor's name in each city, plays Michigan, Ohio, Minnesota, Dakota and Canadian cities.

SAM DOCK SHOWS

Pennsylvanian Sam Dock operated various shows, usually under his name, from about 1887 until 1951, when he was with his grandsons' small show, which was called Sam Dock Circus.

DOWNIE BROS. CIRCUS

Andrew Downie McPhee operated circuses and other tented shows from 1884, traveling by wagon, rail and river boat in various seasons. In 1911-1913 he had Downie & Wheeler Circus; 1914-1917, La Tena Circus; 1918-1924, Walter L. Main Circus, all on rails; then 1926-1930 the Downie Bros. Circus motorized. It was sold in 1930 to Charles Sparks who operated under the Downie name thru 1938. Sold it to other operators for 1939, when it failed and was dispersed.

J. H. ESCHMAN CIRCUS

Traveled about 15 years, disappearing after the 1917 season when its railroad show equipment was auctioned.

FLATFOOT SHOWS

Numerous main-line families around Brewster, New York, were active in this circus syndicate that pioneered much in U.S. circusing. Among their earliest shows was the Zoological Institute, a menagerie, in the 1830s. June, Titus, Angevine, Lent, Crane and other names were associated in the combine that firmly controlled Eastern territory and could make or break rivals. Operated several shows simultaneously in some seasons. George F. Bailey Circus was the last Flatfoot show. It closed in 1875 and The Flatfoots leased the Barnum Circus for two years, then retired.

ADAM FOREPAUGH CIRCUS

Forepaugh began circusing in 1863 and he had a show under his own name from 1866 thru 1890. It was a major show and part of the time it was the nation's biggest. Forepaugh carried on a "white elephant" war in 1884 against the Barnum show. In 1881, he had Louise Montague, winner of a beauty contest his show inspired (and which may have been one of the earliest beauty contests). After Forepaugh's death in 1890, the show was bought by Cooper and Bailey, who continued its operation thru 1894. Bailey then transferred most of the rolling stock to his Buffalo Bill Wild West Show, and the Forepaugh title was combined with that of Sells Bros.

ADAM FOREPAUGH-SELLS BROS. CIRCUS

James A. Bailey, W. W. Cole, and two of the Sells brothers joined forces to operate the Sells equipment to which the Forepaugh name was added. Started in 1896, it was assigned the task, which later failed, of holding Barnum territory against the growing Ringlings while Bailey had the Barnum & Bailey Show touring Europe for five years. In 1905, Bailey acquired full ownership of the show and promptly sold half interest to the Ringlings. The Ringlings acquired full ownership in midseason 1906 and continued to operate the Forepaugh-Sells Circus thru 1908. They revived it for 1910 and 1911 before retiring it permanently. The title was used for legalistic purposes in 1935 on a Ringling subsidiary: Hagenbeck-Wallace & Forepaugh-Sells Bros. Circus.

FRANCONI'S HIPPODROME

Title originated in France, where the Franconi show was an offshoot of the Astley riding show in England. Toured the U.S. in the 1850s.

GAINESVILLE COMMUNITY CIRCUS

Operated by residents of Gainesville, Texas, since it was devised during the Depression as a project to pay off debts of the Little Theater.

GARDEN BROS. CIRCUS

Operated in Canada by William and Ian Garden. The show was founded by their father. It usually has operated as an indoor circus, but in 1957 was to travel as a new tented show.

GENTRY BROS. CIRCUS

Prof. H. B. Gentry expanded a vaudeville dog act into a complete show in 1885 which became a tent show in 1891. Later Prof. Gentry was joined by his brothers and they started a second unit. They bought out a competitor who had two shows, giving them four units. Each carried the Gentry name. At one time, two of the Gentry units were "twins," having identical equipment. By featuring dogs and ponies and catering to women and children, this became a highly successful show. By 1905 the number of units began to decline. In 1907 one unit was leased to the owner of Dan Patch, famous harness horse. Ownership passed to J. Ben Austin and J. D. Newman for 1916-1922. Show was sold to a carnival owner who operated it as Gentry Bros. & James Patterson Circus, 1923-1925. Floyd and Howard King owned a show with the Gentry title from 1926-1929. Sam B. Dill used the name on a truck show in 1930. Original Gentry brothers operated it again, 1931-1934.

GOLLMAR BROS. CIRCUS

Operated by cousins of the Ringlings as a wagon show 1891-1902 and on rails 1903-1916. Other operators had Patterson-Gollmar in 1917 and Gollmar Bros.-Yankee Robinson in 1922.

MIGHTY HAAG CIRCUS

One of the most widely known Southern circuses, starting as a wagon show in the 1890s in Louisiana and continuing for 40 years. It grew steadily thru 1909 when it became a railroad circus, but was losing money by 1914 and returned to wagons after that. First trucks were added in 1918 and the last wagons were replaced in 1929. Motorized show continued in its Southern territory until 1938.

HAGEN BROS. CIRCUS

A motorized tented-show operated by Howard Suesz since 1950.

HAGENBECK-WALLACE CIRCUS

The Hagenbeck name first was known in this country in connection with wild animal acts at theaters, carnivals and world's fairs. The German firm also was known as an animal dealer. After the St. Louis World's Fair of 1904, the family and American showmen joined to build the new Carl Hagenbeck Wild Animal Show, which toured unsuccessfully in

1905 and 1906. The Hagenbecks' U.S. partners sold the show and name to Ben Wallace, who combined it with his Great Wallace Show to create the Hagenbeck-Wallace Circus for 1907. Wallace later sold out. His successors were in charge when the circus train was rammed by a troop train in 1918, a major railroad disaster. The show continued but was sold to the Mugivan and Bowers combination for the 1919 season. They continued with the show thru 1929. It was a Ringling subsidiary, 1930-1935. The 1934 edition was one of the most successful modern circuses and outgrossed its parent Ringling show. The 1935 title was Hagenbeck-Wallace & Forepaugh-Sells Bros. Circus. Ringling didn't operate the show in 1936 and leased it to Howard Y. Bary for 1937-1938, the last time it was on the road.

HAIGHT & DeHAVEN CIRCUS

The DeHaven circus operated from 1861 to 1865, when control was acquired by Andrew Haight. He operated as the Haight & Chambers Circus the next year and lost heavily. Returning to circus business in 1871, Haight resumed a partnership with DeHaven in 1872 and they had the Great Eastern Circus thru 1874, a year when Haight also had the Great Southern Circus. He operated the American Racing Association, an under-canvas hippodrome show, in 1875, and thereafter was employed by other shows.

GEORGE W. HALL SHOWS

A series of small circuses operated in and around Wisconsin from the 1880s, when Popcorn George Hall was in charge, until the 1930s, when his grandchildren were managers.

WILLIAM P. HALL SHOWS

Hall, a Lancaster, Missouri, horse and mule dealer, got into show business by buying stock and equipment of defunct circuses. He then operated a thriving business in used show wagons, horses and, elephants particularly, but leased anything from a single animal to a fully-equipped circus to other showmen. This business gave birth to dozens of shows between 1905-1935, when the remaining usable equipment and the elephants were sold to Cole Bros. Circus.

HAMID-MORTON CIRCUS

A major indoor circus currently in operation. Robert Morton became interested in indoor productions in 1918 when he arranged to rent Gentry Bros. Circus equipment to the Shriners in Dallas. From this start grew the Bob Morton Fraternal Circus. During the Depression this show faltered and Morton was joined by George A. Hamid, a former acrobat with the Buffalo Bill show who had become one of the nation's leading booking agents. The Hamid-Morton partnership subsequently built a powerful route of engagements played annually for Shrine temples, police departments, and others in such cities as Memphis, Milwaukee, Kansas City, Washington, Philadelphia and Toronto.

HARRIS NICKLE PLATE CIRCUS

A small show that was one of the best known among those that charged 10 and 20 cents for admission. It was operated by a Chicago haberdasher 1882-1904, when it was sold to William P. Hall. This put Hall into the used circus business.

HOWES' GREAT LONDON CIRCUS

Started in the 1850s by Seth B. Howes. Toured England 1857-1863 as Howes' Great American Circus and upon its return to this country changed its name to Howes' Great European Circus. Under several ownerships and title variations thru 1870. Returned from a second trip to England in 1871 as the Howes' Great London Circus. Became rail show in 1875 and this was sold to Cooper & Bailey in 1879, whereupon the title and equipment were combined with the Bailey show and eventually combined with Barnum. Meanwhile, other operators resumed use of the original Howes' Great London title on smaller shows in the 20 years prior to 1908. That year the Mugivan and Bowers partnership began use of the name on a railroad show that continued through 1921. The aged Howes title has been used on a few independent circuses since then, the latest one in 1952.

HUNT BROS. CIRCUS

Started in 1892 as Hunt's Vaudeville Circus and continued without interruption to the present time. Charles T. Hunt, the founder, still is active as manager and owner. In 1957 the show toured the Eastern Seaboard.

FRANK JAMES & COLE YOUNGER HISTORIC WILD WEST

The Buckskin Bill Wild West Show under a revised name in 1903 while the infamous outlaws, James and Younger, were with it.

BUCK JONES WILD WEST SHOW

Operated unsuccessfully in 1929 by the cowboy movie star, Buck Jones.

JONES BROTHERS SHOWS

J. Augustus Jones and his brother, Elmer Jones, operated both circuses and tented minstrel shows in profusion. They operated four, six and even more shows at a time. For the most part these were small two-car railroad shows and they were known in turn as King of the Two-Car Shows. Augustus Jones had his first circus in 1892. Among their small shows were Jones Bros. Circus, West & Wells, Great Eastern Hippodrome, Cole & Rogers, Cooper Bros., and King & Tucker. Their larger shows included Cole Bros. Circus, 1916-1918; Buffalo Ranch Wild West and Indian Bill's Wild West. Elmer Jones closed their last circus in 1936 and retired to his Pennsylvania home.

AL G. KELLY & MILLER BROS. CIRCUS

Outgrowth of a very small truck show started by Obert Miller and still a small circus thru 1944. After World War II Miller's sons returned to the show and began expansion which made it one of the most profitable shows on the road. It perfected new types of motorized equipment for circuses, successfully carried giraffes by truck and was first to use an airplane for circus advertising announcements from the air. Its profits increased and rivaled or exceeded those of the Ringling circus in the 1950s. Developed an outstanding menagerie and a large herd of elephants. Currently in operation.

FRANK KETROW SHOWS

Long series of small shows operated from about 1906 until the 1940s under Ketrow, Kay and other titles.

KING BROTHERS SHOWS

Floyd and Howard King left other circus jobs to open their own two-car show in 1919 as Sanger Circus, borrowing the name from the great British circus. Operated as a "car show" (baggage cars and sleepers) thru 1924, when it was the Harris Bros. Circus. In 1925 they switched to flat-car operation and had the Walter L. Main Circus on ten and 15 cars thru 1928, Gentry Bros. Circus on ten or 15 cars, 1926-1929, and ten-car Cole Bros., 1929-1930. Operated other kinds of shows until 1946, when Floyd King established King Bros. Circus, continuing with various partners until 1952, when it became King Bros. & Cristiani Circus. After the name was changed back to King Bros. in 1953, the show toured in 1954 successfully and 1955 unprofitably before folding spectacularly in 1956.

J. H. LaPEARL CIRCUS

Operated out of Danville, Illinois, in the 1890s. Absorbed by the Great Wallace Circus in 1900.

LEE BROS. CIRCUS

A title used by many operators, among them G. W. Christy, Robert Atterbury and Sam Dock. Only rarely has the name been used for more than a year or two at a time and generally there has been no connection between various shows of the same name.

LEMEN BROS. CIRCUS

Opened in 1887 by Frank Lemen and his brothers. They were joined the next year by Martin Downs, who helped build it into a 20-car show. Retitled Great Pan-American Show for a few years. In 1906 its equipment was used for the Hale's Firefighters show. Equipment later reached the William P. Hall farm for resale.

LEWIS B. LENT SHOWS

Lewis B. Lent was an agent for the Flatfoots in 1834. He was a partner in Brown & Lent Circus, a boat show, 1835-1839, and then was associated with Flatfoot shows thru 1842. Lent was a partner in the Rufus Welch National Circus and the Sands & Lent Circus, then partner in Van Amburgh's Menagerie, and June, Titus & Angevine thru the 1840s. After operating more shows with Welch and Howe, he opened L. B. Lent's National Circus, for 1857-1863, and this went on with variations in the name until the New York Circus of 1873-1874. Lent acted as agent or manager for other shows, tried to revive the New York Circus in 1879, and then retired.

COL. TIM McCOY WILD WEST SHOW

Built in 1938 and collapsed after less than one month's operation. Notable as the last major wild west show to troupe after the style of the Buffalo Bill Wild West Show.

MABIE BROS. CIRCUS

Organized in 1840 by Ed and Jere Mabie, with Seth B. Howes as their manager. Relocated in Delavan, Wisconsin, and established that town as a birthplace for many other circuses. Traveled with 50 to 75 horses in the 1850s, playing middlewestern states. Sold out in 1860s, delivering its menagerie to Adam Forepaugh in Chicago on the day Lincoln was shot.

WALTER L. MAIN CIRCUS

Founded in 1885 with seven horses, and was a 90-horse wagon show when sold in 1889 to the Scribner & Smith Circus. Resumed tours in 1890 and went on rails in 1891. Rebuilt after a damaging railroad wreck in 1893. Sold out after the 1899 season but reappeared in 1901. In 1904 the show made its last tour under Main's management, sold its 25-car equipment to William P. Hall and leased the horses to the new Hagenbeck show. Main invested in minor shows in the ensuing years and then leased his name to Andrew Downie, 1918-1924; King brothers, 1925-1928, and other operators, 1930-37.

KEN MAYNARD WILD WEST SHOW

Built for the 1936 season by the Western movie star, Ken Maynard, but lacked finances to get beyond its winter quarters town in California, where performances were given several weekends.

MILLER BROS. 101 RANCH WILD WEST SHOW

Formed in 1908 when Edward Arlington, circusman, and the Millers, Oklahoma ranchers, joined forces with a 16-car show that grew out of a wild west show put on the previous year by Miller cowboys at the Jamestown Exposition. Grew and continued thru 1915, when it featured Jess Willard, boxing champion. In 1916 it was called Buffalo Bill & 101 Ranch Wild West, and Buffalo Bill was among the performers. Arlington bought out the Millers at the end of the season, and with Willard opened it as the Buffalo Bill Wild West & Jess Willard Show in 1917. Buffalo Bill had died. Willard bought the show and it folded. In 1925 the Millers re-entered the business with a 30-car wild west show under the 101 Ranch name. It folded in 1931. Title was revived on a small show in 1945-46.

MILLS BROS. CIRCUS

Opened in 1940 as a small truck show by three brothers who had been employed by other shows. They adapted and developed a system of using local sponsors to insure ticket sales, and the show thrived. Currently in operation.

TOM MIX CIRCUS

Tom Mix, Western star, had an interest in the Sam B. Dill Circus & Tom Mix Wild West of 1934. In 1935 he owned the show and renamed it the Tom Mix Circus. It failed in 1938. Mix performed in several wild west shows before going into movies, and was a major feature with the Sells Floto Circus before starting his own show.

MONTGOMERY QUEEN CIRCUS

Bought equipment from Forepaugh in 1873 and sold out in 1878 after successfully touring the Far West.

HONEST BILL NEWTON CIRCUS

Lucky Bill Newton was a show owner who had been active on the Western frontier and then took small circuses into the Rockies. He continued active until about the time of World War I. Meanwhile, his son, Honest Bill Newton, also entered circus business and had small shows under his own name and other titles operating out of Quenemo, Kansas. The third generation, Clyde Newton, started circusing in the 1920s. They had Orange Bros., Moon Bros., Newton Bros., Honest Bill Circus and other shows thru 1938, and had interests in minor circuses in later years.

NORRIS & ROWE CIRCUS

Began as a dog and pony show at the turn of the century and quickly grew to 20 and 25-car size. Toured Mexico as well as the western states. Folded shortly after opening the 1910 season.

JOHN O'BRIEN CIRCUS

Entered circus business in 1861 by renting horses to a show which he subsequently owned. At various times he had the Dan Rice Circus, was a partner with Forepaugh, managed the Barnum show and operated four of his own shows simultaneously. His fortunes dimmed and he had small shows in years just prior to his death in 1889.

ORTON BROS. CIRCUS

The Orton family started in circus operation with Hiram Orton, Great Lakes sailor who opened his show in 1854. Upon his retirement in 1862, the show was continued by his son, Miles Orton, thru 1895. He and a brother, R. Z. Orton, had Orton Bros. Circus until 1898, when they split into two Orton circuses. One or both then was on the road until Miles' death in 1903. R. Z. Orton continued as a small show, except for 1916 when the Ortons tried their luck with a minor railroad show. That failed and the old wagon show was reopened. It became a truck show in the 1920s and lasted until the early 1930s. The show had become one of the great names among small shows. Several members of the family continued as performers with other shows.

TOM PACKS CIRCUS

From successful promotion of boxing and wrestling bouts, Tom Packs began production of rodeos in St. Louis. Thru this connection and promotion of appearances by cowboy movie stars, Packs became interested in circus production. In 1937 he began presenting a circus show in front of grandstands and in ball parks. By 1941 this show was well established, and since then it has played sponsored dates regularly in open stadiums, ball parks and some indoor arenas. In 1956 it added a second unit to play Western territory.

PARKER & WATTS CIRCUS

Motorized circus of 1938-1939.

PAWNEE BILL'S WILD WEST

Operated by Major Gordon (Pawnee Bill) Lillie in a style similar to that of the Buffalo Bill Wild West Show. It toured Europe as well as the U.S. and Canada in the 1890s. After the 1907 season it sold its wagons and train to circuses and appeared all of 1908 at an amusement park. Lillie then bought into the Buffalo Bill show and for the period 1909-1913 it was entitled the Buffalo Bill Wild West & Pawnee Bill Great Far East Show. Nicknamed the Two Bills show, it collapsed in 1913. Pawnee Bill later tried several comebacks, including several shows that were planned but never materialized, and a wild west show on a carnival in the 1930s. But these never approximated the original.

POLACK BROS. CIRCUS

The Polack brothers operated important railroad carnivals in the 1920s but the depression closed these and I. J. Polack became agent for the Milt Holland Indoor Circus. Holland operated only in the winter and Polack, together with Louis Stern, took over the same organization to run in the summer as the Eastern States Circus. This became Polack Bros. Circus and played sponsored indoor dates. By the mid-1940s it had offers of more dates than it could accept, so a second unit was formed. Both Polack units continued thru 1957 as major circuses.

DAN RICE CIRCUS

This circus probably was the prototype of the circus described by Mark Twain in *Huckleberry Finn* and it is believed to have been the show which infected five young customers named Ringling with the circus fever. The show owner reportedly inspired the cartoonists' version of Uncle Sam; he used his show to campaign for Zachary Taylor, to become friendly with Abraham Lincoln and to further his own urge to be President. Dan Rice gained fame as a clown on other shows and formed his own company in 1848, traveling by Mississippi riverboat. Rice became the most famous and popular performer of his time, comparing with today's most acclaimed film and TV stars. The Dan Rice Circus continued successfully in the 1850s and its owners' friends included Horace Greeley, Jefferson Davis and Robert E. Lee. In 1861-2, in the South, he appeared to side with the Confederacy and caused a near-riot when his show reappeared in the North. Frequently, he closed his own circus and became the star of another. Sometimes, his show was owned by others but featured him. Forepaugh owned the Rice circus in 1865 and 1866. Rice had other partners and angels until 1881, by which time his lack of dependability ruined him. After his death in 1900 other showmen used his name. There was a Rice circus in 1901; Rice Bros. Circus, 1909-1914; other Rice shows in 1923, 1934-7, 1945 and a Dan Rice Circus unit on a carnival in 1954-1955.

R. T. RICHARDS CIRCUS

Named by reversing the name of its owner, Richard T. Ringling, son of Alf T. Ringling. It operated in 1917 as a wagon show with a number of motor trucks.

RICKETTS CIRCUS

Generally acknowledged as the first full circus to perform in the United States, this was an indoor show which appeared in special buildings at Philadelphia and New York in 1793 and 1794. In the next year it also exhibited at Boston, Salem and other cities, some of them in Canada. Late in 1799 fires razed the Ricketts buildings at both Philadelphia and New York, folding the show. Its owner, John Bill Ricketts, a rider, appeared then with another show and subsequently was lost at sea.

RING BROS. CIRCUS

A current circus operated by Franco Richards and playing smaller towns in the East and South.

RINGLING BROS. CIRCUS

Began at Baraboo, Wisconsin, in 1884, after the Ringlings had toured several winters with a comic concert company in which they appeared. Yankee Robinson helped them start. The show grew steadily. It bought its first elephants in 1888, leased the Van Amburg name for a subtitle in 1889, went on rails in 1890, first played Chicago in 1895, battled for territory against Bailey's shows (Barnum & Bailey, Buffalo Bill, Forepaugh-Sells) in 1896, and first went to the West Coast in 1899. When Barnum & Bailey went to Europe for five years, Forepaugh-Sells Circus was left to hold the Eastern cities against competition, but Ringling Bros. Circus won out in the highly competitive and combative struggle. Equalled Barnum & Bailey in size and surpassed it in operation in 1903-07. Bought Forepaugh-Sells Circus in 1906 and operated it as a subsidiary thru 1907 and again in 1910-11. Bought Barnum & Bailey Circus and operated it as a separate show, 1908-1918. Combined with Barnum & Bailey to form the Ringling Bros. and Barnum & Bailey Circus in 1919.

RINGLING BROS. AND BARNUM & BAILEY CIRCUS

The Greatest Show on Earth. Created by combining the Barnum & Bailey Circus with Ringling Bros. Circus in 1919 and operated by the Ringlings on from 70 to more than 100 railroad cars. Opened each year at Madison Square Garden, New York. Quartered first at Bridgeport, Connecticut, and then at Sarasota, Florida. In 1929, only days before the stock market crash, John Ringling bought the American Circus Corp., which included five major circuses. Depression years wiped out these subsidiaries and weakened the Ringling-Barnum show to the point where bankers appointed Samuel Gompertz as manager. John Ringling, last of the original brothers, died in 1936. A nephew, John Ringling North, won control of the show for the family again in 1938 and soon the family factions began bickering. The show survived a strike in 1938, disastrous fire in 1944 and such lesser blows as the poisoning of 11 elephants, difficulties of wartime travel, and the in-family fight for control. In 1956 the circus closed in mid-season and North announced it would thereafter appear only in buildings and not in a tent. It began in 1957 as an indoor show.

ROBBINS BROS. CIRCUS

Fred Buchanan's World Bros. Circus of 1923 was renamed Robbins Bros. Circus in 1924. This operated as a railroad show until 1931. The title was used by others on various motorized shows in depression years and on another railroad show in 1938. It last appeared in 1949 on a truck show.

BURR ROBBINS CIRCUS

Operated from 1871 thru 1888 out of Wisconsin. In later years Robbins financed other circuses. His son and grandson became executives in the outdoor advertising business.

FRANK A. ROBBINS CIRCUS

Robbins, a protege of Adam Forepaugh, operated a railroad show, 1881-1891. After it failed Robbins recouped and reopened his show for 1905-1915.

FAMOUS ROBINSON CIRCUS

Operated 1910-1912 by Dan Robinson. The show was purchased by Mugivan and Bowers so that they could use the Robinson name in the territory of John Robinson Circus. They did this thru 1915 but after that season they bought the original John Robinson Circus and discontinued the Famous Robinson Circus.

JOHN ROBINSON CIRCUS

Claimed to have been started in 1824 but probably began about 1840, by the first of four generations of John Robinsons. Became a major circus and a household word in the South. Went on rails in 1881. Sometimes the title was varied thru addition of a partner's name, but ultimately it was known as John Robinson's Ten Big Shows. Leased by the Ringlings and managed by Henry Ringling for 1898 only. Robinsons resumed control in 1899 and continued thru 1911. Off the road, 1912-1915. Purchased by Mugivan and Bowers for 1916. They resold the original Robinson equipment and retained only the show name, operating it and other equipment until 1929. Ringling again operated John Robinson Circus in 1930. The title was used in connection with the Sells Floto Circus of 1932 and with the Al G. Barnes-Sells Floto Circus of 1938 as a secondary title.

YANKEE ROBINSON CIRCUS

Initiated in 1854. For several early years it gave a circus in the afternoons and "Uncle Tom's Cabin" at nights, becoming the first of hundreds of tent shows to give "Uncle Tom." Had two units in 1858 and the Number 2 show was probably the first to feed and house all personnel on the show grounds rather than in hotels. In 1859, Yankee Robinson's title offended Southerners while he was in the Carolinas and he fled from a mob, abandoning all equipment. In 1860-64 he effected a comeback, and he had a big wagon show, 1865-1869. In the latter year the show took in more money than any other show up to that time. But Yankee had two units in 1870 and both lost money. By 1876 he had lost his show again. Robinson operated dramatic shows until 1884 when he was retained as adviser by the Ringlings for their first circus. This was called The Yankee Robinson & Ringling Bros. Great Double Shows, Circus and Caravan. Robinson died during the season, and his name was not used on a circus again until 1905-1920, when Fred Buchanan had a Yankee Robinson Circus. Equipment and title then were sold to the Mugivan and Bowers combination. It was a subtitle on the Gollmar Bros. Circus of 1922.

ROWE'S CALIFORNIA CIRCUS

California's first circus was started by Joseph A. Rowe, equestrian, who opened in a San Francisco theater on October 29, 1849, during the gold rush. The show later played the mining towns in the interior and in the 1850s made two voyages to the South Seas, touring Australia and Hawaii. Operated under various titles: Rowe's Olympic Circus, Rowe's American Circus (in Australia), Rowe and Smith's Circus, etc. Pioneer Rowe returned to San Francisco in 1860 after an unprofitable trip to the South Seas and closed his show. For many years thereafter he was with several circuses as rider, ringmaster and advance agent.

RUSSELL BROS. CIRCUS

Operated in the 1920s by Mr. and Mrs. C. W. Webb, who built it into an important motorized circus in the 1930s. Played the middle west until 1941, when it moved its quarters and route to California. Opened in Los Angeles in 1942. Sold to Arthur Concello for 1943. Combined into the Clyde Beatty & Russell Bros. Circus for 1944. Transformed into a railroad show for 1945, when it was Russell Bros. Pan-Pacific Circus, and sold to Clyde Beatty before the 1946 season.

SANGER'S GREAT EUROPEAN CIRCUS

The title originated with Lord George Sanger in Great Britain, but the American shows to use the name were not connected with the original. Mugivan & Bowers partnership bought the Dode Fisk Circus and called it Sanger Circus for 1911-1913. When Mugivan-Bowers bought the Danny Robinson title, the Sanger show was repainted over a weekend and thereafter called the Robinson show. Other Americans also have used the Sanger name.

SIG SAUTELLE CIRCUS

A ventriloquist, Sautelle opened his own circus in 1885 on wagons. It went on rails, 1902-1905, and then see-sawed between wagons and rails for the next several years, closing in 1919.

SEILS-STERLING CIRCUS

Grew out of the Lindemann Bros. Circus of the 1920s and was a major motorized circus in the 1930s. Equipment sold in 1938.

SELLS BROS. CIRCUS

Started in 1872 as Paul Silverburg Circus by four Sells brothers of Columbus, and called Sells Bros. Circus in 1875. In 1878, the wagon show was retitled and a new railroad show was assembled under the Sells name. Billed in 1884 as the Sells Bros. 50-Cage 4-Ring Circus. Reached 45-car size in 1885, when it also had a subsidiary with 44 cars. Catered to Mid-Western farm communities. In 1896 the Sells equipment was renamed Forepaugh-Sells Circus, and two of the Sells brothers, with James A. Bailey and W. W. Cole, owned the show.

WILLIE SELLS SHOWS

Adopted son of one of the Sells brothers, Willie Sells was first a performer and later an owner. Titles of shows in which he was involved included Sells & Andress, 1889; Sells & Renfew, 1892-1894; Great Syndicate Shows, 1895-6; Sells & Gray, 1900-01; Sells & Downs, 1902-1905, and others.

SELLS FLOTO CIRCUS

Owners of the Denver *Post* started the Floto Dog & Pony Show in 1902. Enlarging it and wanting a fuller title in 1906, they brought Willie Sells into the firm and called the show Sells Floto Circus. Since the Sells title was owned by the Ringlings, Sells Floto was sued in 1909 and was ordered not to use the pictures of original Sells brothers. In 1913, owners of Sells Floto Circus figured in the financial failure of the Buffalo Bill Wild West Show, and in 1914-15 their name was Sells Floto-Buffalo Bill Circus, with Buffalo Bill as a feature. From 1921 until the end of 1929 the show was owned by Mugivan and Bowers' American Circus Corporation. Ringling bought the company and operated Sells Floto in 1930-1932. The title was appended to the Al G. Barnes Circus for 1937 and 1938, its last appearance.

SPALDING & ROGERS CIRCUS

Started in the 1840s as a wagon show, this combination built the Floating Palace, deluxe riverboat designed as a floating arena in which circus performances were given. The show gained its fame as a boat-show on the Ohio and Mississippi in the 1850s. "Dr." Gilbert Spalding featured Dan Rice several times, but they became enemies and rivals, carrying on a bitter fight with their circuses. Spalding & Rogers Floating Palace was completely burned at New Albany, Indiana, in 1865.

SPARKS CIRCUS

The circus man's circus, Sparks was started as the John H. Sparks Old Virginia Shows in the 1890s, touring the South on wagons. Was two-car show at the turn of the century and on seven rail cars by 1909. In 1916 the show was on 15 cars and Charles Sparks, the adopted son of John H., was manager. Showmen came to look upon the Sparks Circus as an ideal organization and upon Charles Sparks as a leading manager. Show was on 20 cars thru the 1920s. Sparks sold his show after the 1928 season but did not realize the true buyer was the American Circus Corp. This firm had the show in 1929 and then sold it to Ringling, which continued it for 1930 and 1931. Charles Sparks, meanwhile, bought and operated the Downie circus. Ringling leased the Sparks name for use on a show that was motorized in 1946 and on rails in 1947.

STONE & MURRAY CIRCUS

Den Stone, clown and rider, started his own show about 1861 in a partnership called Stone, Rosston & Co. Circus. It became Stone, Rosston & Murray when John H. Murray joined in 1864. The next season this show was first to tour the South after the Civil War. Rosston dropped out and it was Stone & Murray Circus, 1866-1875. After Stone quit, it went on as John H. Murray Circus thru 1878.

SUN BROS. CIRCUS

Opened in 1892 under direction of George, Peter and Gus Sun. Moved on nine railroad cars thru most of its seasons and generally stayed in the Southeast and East. Gus Sun left the organization to start a minstrel show, another circus, and later a theater from which sprang the famous Sun vaudeville circuit. The other brothers continued the circus successfully until they sold out in 1918.

THAYER & NOYES CIRCUS

"Dr." James Thayer was a highly successful clown and Charles Noyes was a capable trainer. As youths each worked with various circuses. Together they comprised the strength of the Dan Rice Circus about 1860. The following year each had a show of his own, Noyes leasing the Rice show. From 1862 until 1869 they had the Thayer & Noyes Circus in successful operation. They were caught up in the disastrous circus season of 1869, when only six of 28 shows lasted out the season, and Thayer & Noyes Circus was sold at auction. Noyes had the C. W. Noyes Crescent City Circus, 1869-1874. Thayer represented P. T. Barnum on the Barnum show that was leased to O'Brien. In 1877 and 1879 Thayer had small shows of his own.

ARON TURNER CIRCUS

Started in the 1830s, the Aron Turner Circus was one of the first tented circuses in the United States. In 1836, one employee was P. T. Barnum, then a young man getting his first taste of circusing, and another was George F. Bailey. Bailey went on to become Turner's son-in-law and ultimate owner of the circus. Under Bailey's guidance it was linked with the Flatfoot group and eventually named the George F. Bailey Circus.

VAN AMBURGH CIRCUS

Isaac Van Amburgh was the first important American wild animal trainer. He first appeared as a feature of Flatfoot shows and later started his own circus and menagerie. From 1846 thru 1883 the manager of Van Amburgh Circus was Hyatt Frost, a leading showman who continued successfully after death of Van Amburgh in 1865. The show was reluctant to give up wagons for trains and was one of the last major circuses to make the change. Frost revived the title in 1885, then leased the name to Ringling Bros. Circus as a subtitle in 1889. Other shows also picked up the name. In 1904 Jerry Mugivan and Bert Bowers started their circus empire with a small rail show they called Van Amburgh, and it continued until mid-year of 1908. At that time the show's name was changed to Howes' Great London Circus. The name Van Amburgh again was relegated to substitle status and soon disappeared.

VON BROS. CIRCUS

A circus operated by Henry Vonderheid in Eastern states.

GREAT WALLACE SHOWS

Started by Al G. Fields, who later became the top name in minstrels, James Anderson, and Ben Wallace in 1884 at Peru, Indiana, and put on rails in 1886. Wallace gained full control in 1887. The show was operated as Cook & Whitby circus for 1892-1894, but resumed the Wallace name for 1895 and thereafter. After the 1906 season Wallace bought the Hagenbeck show and combined the two in 1907 to form Hagenbeck-Wallace Circus.

LEON W. WASHBURN SHOWS

Washburn was manager and later owner of the Stetson Uncle Tom's Cabin shows, then formed his own circus in 1881. This continued under a variety of titles until about 1908, when he bought a theater. Periodically, he returned to the road with either a circus, carnival or "Uncle Tom's Cabin" show thru 1925.

WELSH BROS. CIRCUS

Operated 1890 thru 1915 by the Welshes out of Lancaster, Pennsylvania. Sold to Al F. Wheeler.

A. F. WHEELER SHOWS

Started in 1893 when Wheeler and Sam Dock left Welsh Bros. Combined with Downie for the Downie & Wheeler Circus of 1911-1913. Had Wheeler Bros. Circus in 1914-1916, then 1921-22. Wheeler operated or managed shows of various titles thru 1930, when he had Al F. Wheeler Circus again. Then followed the Wheeler & Sautelle Circus 1931-32; Al F. Wheeler Circus and Tiger Bill Wild West, 1932, and Wheeler & Almond Circus, 1933.

TOM WIEDEMANN SHOWS

Operated Wiedemann Bros. Big American Shows, 1908-1910; Kit Carson Wild West Show, 1911-1914; Barton & Bailey Circus, 1915.

YOUNG BUFFALO BILL WILD WEST SHOW

Operated 1910-1914.

Credits and References

Abbreviations: N.Y.P.L. New York Public Library
S.A.P.L. Harry Hertzberg Circus Collection, San Antonio Public Library

Jacket: Harry Hertzberg Circus Collection, San Antonio Public Library (S.A.P.L. hereafter)
Title page, left S.A.P.L.

PAGE POSITION		PAGE POSITION		PAGE POSITION	
2	Metropolitan Museum of Art, New York	20	from *Natural History Magazine*, 1933	38	Museum of the City of New York
3 all three	New York Public Library (N.Y.P.L. hereafter)	21 top, left	N.Y.P.L.	39 top	Harvard College Library, Theatre Collection
		bottom, left	S.A.P.L.		
4 top	N.Y.P.L.	right	Harvard College Library, Theatre Collection	bottom	N.Y.P.L.
bottom	Museum of the American Circus, Sarasota	22	Metropolitan Museum of Art	40	*Illustrated London Times*, June 1861
5 top	Painting by F. Matania	23 top	N.Y.P.L., Theatre Collection	41	*Vanity Fair*, June 9, 1860
bottom	N.Y.P.L.			42 & 43	Harvard College Library, Theatre Collection
6 & 7	Painting by Jean Leon Gerome, courtesy Racquet and Tennis Club, N.Y.	bottom	S.A.P.L.		
		24 both	Peabody Museum, Salem, Mass.	44 top, left	Robert D. Good, Allentown, Pa.
8 top	N.Y.P.L.	25 left	New York Historical Society	top, right	S.A.P.L.
bottom, both	from *Old England* by Charles Knight			bottom	Robert D. Good
		right	Nat Green	45 & 46	S.A.P.L.
9 top, both	N.Y.P.L.	26 top	New York Historical Society	47 top	Museum of the City of New York
bottom, both	from *Circus Parade* by John S. Clarke	bottom	S.A.P.L.	bottom	S.A.P.L.
10 top	N.Y.P.L.	27	American Antiquarian Society, Worcester, Mass.	48 both	S.A.P.L.
bottom, both	from *Old England*			49	New York Historical Society
11 top	N.Y.P.L., Theatre Collection	28	Authors' Collection	50	S.A.P.L.
bottom	N.Y.P.L.	29	Harvard College Library, Theatre Collection	51 top	S.A.P.L.
12 & 13	from *Trois Dialogues De L'Exercise De Savater*			bottom	Museum of the American Circus
14 top	Museum of the American Circus	30	*Life*, May 13, 1920	52 top	Museum of the American Circus
		31 left	Harvard College Library, Theatre Collection		
bottom, all	N.Y.P.L.			bottom	S.A.P.L.
15 top two and bottom, left	from *Old England*	right	American Antiquarian Society	53 top	Museum of the City of New York
bottom, right	Museum of the American Circus	32	Harvard College Library, Theatre Collection	bottom	S.A.P.L.
16 both	N.Y.P.L., Theatre Collection	33 top	N.Y.P.L., Theatre Collection	54 top	The Alice Curtis Desmond Collection, Barnum Museum, Bridgeport, Conn.
17 top	S.A.P.L.	bottom	New York Historical Society	bottom, both	S.A.P.L.
bottom	Museum of the American Circus	34-36 all	from *California's Pioneer Circus*, courtesy H. S. Crocker, Inc., San Francisco	55	New York Historical Society
18 top	Museum of the American Circus			56 top, left	L. W. Jenkins Collection, Peabody Museum
bottom	N.Y.P.L., Theatre Collection			top, right	Museum of the American Circus
19 top	S.A.P.L.	37	S.A.P.L.	bottom, left	S.A.P.L.
bottom	Museum of the American Circus				

PAGE POSITION

56 bottom, right — L. W. Jenkins Collection, Peabody Museum
57 top — N.Y.P.L.
   bottom — S.A.P.L.
58 top, left — Museum of the American Circus
   top, right — Elizabeth Sterling Seeley Collection, Barnum Museum
   bottom — S.A.P.L.
59 — S.A.P.L.
60 top — S.A.P.L.
   bottom — N.Y.P.L., Print Room
61 — S.A.P.L.
62 & 63 — New York Historical Society
64 & 65 — Harvard College Library, Theatre Collection
66 — Headline, New York Historical Association
   top — *Harper's Weekly*, Dec. 4, 1869
   bottom — New York Historical Association
67 top — Harvard College Library, Theatre Collection
   bottom — S.A.P.L.
68 — New York Historical Society
69 — S.A.P.L.
70 — Library of Congress
71 both — S.A.P.L.
72 top — Strobridge Lithographing Co.
   bottom — S.A.P.L.
73 top — S.A.P.L.
   bottom — Library of Congress
74 & 75 — S.A.P.L.
76 top — Princeton University, McCaddon Collection
   bottom — S.A.P.L.
77 — Strobridge Lithographing Co.
78 — S.A.P.L.
79 top — *Life*, May 30, 1889
   bottom — Library of Congress
80 both — Library of Congress
81-83 all — S.A.P.L.
84 top — Harvard College Library, Theatre Collection
   bottom — S.A.P.L.
85 top — Library of Congress
   bottom — S.A.P.L.
86 & 87 — S.A.P.L.
88 top — Harvard College Library, Theatre Collection
   bottom — S.A.P.L.
89 — S.A.P.L.
90 top — N.Y.P.L., Theatre Collection
   bottom — S.A.P.L.
91-93 all — S.A.P.L.

94 — Strobridge Lithographing Co.
95 — Princeton University, McCaddon Collection
96 top — S.A.P.L.
   bottom — Museum of the American Circus
97 both — S.A.P.L.
98 — S.A.P.L.
99 top — Library of Congress
   bottom — Princeton University, McCaddon Collection
100 — Harvard College Library, Theatre Collection
101 all — Peabody Museum
102 top — S.A.P.L.
   bottom — Courtesy Alton Hall Blackington
103 & 104 — New York Historical Society
105 top, both — S.A.P.L.
   bottom — Princeton University, McCaddon Collection
106 top, both — S.A.P.L.
   bottom — Circus Hall of Fame, Sarasota
107 both — S.A.P.L.
108 top — from *Tattoo* by Albert Parry, courtesy Simon & Schuster
   bottom — S.A.P.L.
109 — Harvard College Library Theatre Collection
110 & 111 all — S.A.P.L.
112 top, left — Peabody Museum, courtesy L. W. Jenkins
   top, right — S.A.P.L.
   bottom — S.A.P.L.
113 top — from the *Scientific American*, Dec. 12, 1891
   bottom — Museum of the City of New York
114 & 115 — New York Historical Society
116 all — S.A.P.L.
117 top — S.A.P.L.
   bottom, left — Princeton University, McCaddon Collection
   bottom, right — S.A.P.L.
118 top — S.A.P.L.
   bottom — from *Cosmopolitan*, 1908
119 — New York Historical Society
120 — S.A.P.L.
121 top (l. & r.) — Robert D. Good
   top, center — S.A.P.L.
   bottom — Robert D. Good
122 top, left — S.A.P.L.
   top, right — Princeton University, McCaddon Collection
   bottom, left — S.A.P.L.
   bottom, right — Princeton University, McCaddon Collection

123 top, both — Princeton University, McCaddon Collection
   bottom — S.A.P.L.
124 top, both — Brown Bros., N. Y.
   bottom — S.A.P.L.
125 top — Museum of the City of New York
   bottom, left — S.A.P.L.
   bottom, right — Brown Bros.
126 & 127 — *Puck*, Oct. 29, 1878
128 & 129 — Knickerbocker Pictures, N. Y.
130 — Library of Congress
131 — S.A.P.L.
132 both — N.Y.P.L.
133 both — *Puck*, April 13, 1887
134 both — S.A.P.L.
135 top — S.A.P.L.
   bottom — N.Y.P.L., photo by Dudley, Hartford, Conn.
136-139 all — S.A.P.L.
140 — Harvard College Library, Theatre Collection
141 & 142 — S.A.P.L.
143 & 144 all — Alice Durant
145 — Library of Congress
146 top — Courtesy Henry Ringling North
   bottom — *Harper's Bazaar*, July 12, 1873
147 top — Courtesy Henry Ringling North
   bottom, both — from *Life Story of the Ringling Brothers*
148 top — from *Life Story of the Ringling Brothers*
   bottom, left — Museum of the City of New York
   bottom, right — from *Life Story of the Ringling Brothers*
149 top — S.A.P.L.
   bottom — Courtesy Henry Ringling North
150 top — from *Century Magazine*, 1905
   bottom — from *Harper's Bazaar*, Jan. 22, 1887
151 top — Library of Congress
   bottom — N.Y.P.L.
152 all — Princeton University, McCaddon Collection
153 — Princeton University, McCaddon Collection
154 — S.A.P.L.
155 top — Strobridge Lithographing Co.
   bottom — S.A.P.L.
156 both — Robert D. Good
157 both — Library of Congress
158 both — Princeton University, McCaddon Collection
159 top — S.A.P.L.
   bottom — Princeton University, McCaddon Collection

Index